Space Invaders

Space Invaders

Race, Gender and Bodies Out of Place

Nirmal Puwar

Oxford • New York

First published in 2004 by
Berg
Editorial offices:
1st Floor, Angel Court, 81 St Clements Street, Oxford OX4 1AW, UK
175 Fifth Avenue, New York, NY 10010, USA

© Nirmal Puwar 2004

Berg is the imprint of Oxford International Publishers Ltd.

Library of Congress Cataloging-in-Publication Data
A catalogue record for this book is available from the Library of Congress.

British Library Cataloguing-in-Publication Data
A catalogue record for this book is available from the British Library.

ISBN 1 85973 654 8 (Cloth)
1 85973 659 9 (Paper)

Typeset by JS Typesetting Ltd, Wellingborough, Northants.
Printed in the United Kingdom by Biddles Ltd, King's Lynn.

www.bergpublishers.com

For my parents, Kartar Kaur
and Sawarn Singh

Contents

Acknowledgements

It is difficult to mention all the people who have contributed to the making of this book. The quiet encouragement of my family and most especially my parents has played a very important role in sustaining me through all of my scholarly expeditions. John Scott has provided academic support for funding, writing and publishing the research. Several friends and colleagues have read drafts and engaged in discussions that have contributed to the final work. In alphabetical order they are: Stephania Abrar, Avtar Brah, Pankesh Chandarana, Howard Feather, Miriam Glucksman, Catherine Hall, John Hoffman, Steven Loyal, Charles Mills, Daljit Nagra, Julia O'Connell-Davidson, Carole Pateman, Anne Phillips, Andy Pilkington, Helen Rainbird, Vicky Randall, Teresa Sacchet and Sanjay Sharma.

The thought and consideration of the one hundred MPs and senior civil servants I interviewed must be fully acknowledged. After all, it was these conversations that set me thinking in the direction of the analysis that frames this book. The ESRC funded this research on 'New and Established Elites' (project no. R00023545, Directed by John Scott at Essex University).

The research that this book pulls together has been presented at numerous conferences and seminars (too many to mention here). I am thankful to all those colleagues who have waited patiently for the core of those presentations to appear in this book. I have no doubt tried the patience of Kathryn Earle; I appreciate all the time and effort Berg have granted me. And here I would like to thank the copy editor Margaret Last, Ian Critchley in Production and Caroline McCarthy in Editorial.

I am most grateful to the artists who have granted me permission to use their work – Anish Kapoor, Antony Gormley and Jane and Louise Wilson. Justyna Niewara from the Lisson Gallery and Sophie Greig from the White Cube have been especially helpful in attaining these images. Atlantic Symcation have enabled me to use David Low's cartoon. Wendy Woods from the Nelson Mandela Statue Fund has been especially supportive.

Introduction: Proximities

The language of diversity is today embraced as a holy mantra across different sites. We are told that diversity is good for us. It makes for an enriched multicultural society. There is a business case for diversity. There is a governance case for diversity. Within these loud proclamations, what diversity actually is remains muffled in the sounds of celebration and social inclusion. In policy terms, diversity has overwhelmingly come to mean the inclusion of different bodies. It is assumed that, once we have more women and racialised minorities, or other groups, represented in the hierarchies of organisations (government, civil service, judiciary, police, universities and the arts sector), especially in the élite positions of those hierarchies, then we shall have diversity. Structures and policies will become much more open when these groups enter and make a difference to organisations.

The arrival of women and racialised minorities in spaces from which they have been historically or conceptually excluded is an illuminating and intriguing paradox. It is illuminating because it sheds light on how spaces have been formed through what has been constructed out. And it is intriguing because it is a moment of change. It disturbs the status quo, while at the same time bearing the weight of the sedimented past. This book takes this altered moment as its point of departure. It asks what happens when those bodies not expected to occupy certain places do so. And most specifically it is concerned to ask what happens when women and racialised minorities take up 'privileged' positions which have not been 'reserved' for them, for which, they are not, in short, the somatic norm. What are the terms of coexistence? This is an encounter that causes disruption, necessitates negotiation and invites complicity. Here we have the paradox of the increasing proximity of the hitherto outside with the inside proper, or, should I say, with the somatic norm. While they now exist on the inside, they still do not have an undisputed right to occupy the space.

Even the most historically protected spaces can't be contained. They remain dynamic and open to other possibilities. Space is not a fixed entity. 'It moves and changes, depending on how it is used, what is done with and to it, and how open it is to even further changes' (Grosz 2001: 7). The homogenisation of space is thus contradictory, as space carries properties which are simultaneously open to transformation, just as much as they are sedimented.

The Openness of Dynamic Space

Trafalgar Square has and continues to be a place from where the British nation is celebrated (in ritual, stone and ceremony). But it has also been the site of protest and demonstration. Right from the feet of Nelson's Column, in whose honour the square was laid between 1830 and 1845 to commemorate the Admiral's naval victory at the Battle of Trafalgar (off the Spanish coast) in 1805, representing the superior might of the seafaring British nation, political speeches have addressed angry crowds. Political demands have hollered past the domineering 185-foot column, from where Nelson looks down Whitehall towards Admiralty. A rally that ends here after a long day of marching represents a high point, something between a crescendo and a finale. Thus it is no surprise that the police often buckle up, become tense and anxious and have been known to panic in anticipation of what the final reckoning with the symbolic pillars of power will entail. It is certainly a place from where new publics are made and the unexpected can prevail.

On 17 November 2001 thousands of anti-war protesters, who had marched from Hyde Park and past the Ritz on Piccadilly, against the pending attack on Afghanistan as a response to 9/11, poured into the square to hear the political speeches. But first, at sunset, with a red hue in the sky encircling the square, the Ramadan fast was broken, and the square was transformed. The sepulchral sound of *namaz* flowed through Trafalgar Square. This distinguished site of both political protest and national monument mutated in both senses. Framed by embassies to the east (South Africa House) and the west (Canada House), these vast reminders of imperial splendour, it is topped from on high by the mighty National Gallery and its grand doors. Standing in the desperate shadows of a pending war, the imperial square provided perfect acoustic properties for Muslim prayers. The Arabic sounds reverberated off the heavy tonnage which flank the four corners with ceremonial stone into the bodies of a disparate gathering of a public.

The four gargantuan bronze lions (designed by Landseer) protecting Nelson were subjected to not only an echo that belied heads of states, international agencies and the military–industrial complex, but also a wail that spoke with a postcolonial accent. The sounds of a call overwhelmingly, most especially after 9/11, associated with demonic fundamentalism stirred between the bodies of a multiply diverse crowd. For a fleeting moment, people of all religions, ages, classes and incommensurable political allegiances were, in an unimaginable way, a collectivity. As the *namaz* traversed the crowd, they stood in silence and this public space was produced anew. The proscribed sound upset predictable readings of both nation and accepted idioms of protest. The foreign exclaim and the gathering of a broad and multiple mass of thousands in the most famous and politicised square in history, steeped in Empire, created an altogether different echo.

Both the international and the national have been intimately constitutive of this local landmark of London, England and Britain. The concerted attempt to set the history of the nation in stone threatened to come apart in a re-routing of how the international is constituted from within the square. Both the sound and the gathering opened up for interrogation how global relations have been figured right from within Trafalgar. This was a presence whose hue lit up the consecrated space and held it up for questioning. Sedimented structures became movable – porous, open, dynamic, fluid and subject to transformation. The combined properties of the purpose of this huge gathering, which pleaded with a British government on the brink of bombarding Afghanistan, the sound amidst the red light of the sky, illuminated the imperial power of the square, which was itself up for a new reckoning.

The Consecrated Somatic Norm

There are plans to bring another Nelson to the square, a bronze statue of Nelson Mandela. While the naval hero faces his Admiralty, and the equestrian statue of Charles I faces Banqueting House, from where he stepped to the scaffold for his execution in 1649, Mandela, it is hoped, will face the South African embassy, from the spot where anti-apartheid protesters called out for change. Ken Livingstone (the current Mayor of London) has provocatively claimed that the two Nelsons will mark the shift from Empire to a multicultural society.

Perhaps being symptomatic of how a multicultural society does not automatically become a multicultural nation, Mandela's statue has been a contested phenomenon. The pending arrival of a 'black'[1] figure of leadership in this privileged public domain, reserved for very specific types of heroes, has raised a revealing dispute. The coupling of particular bodies with specific spaces is at the heart of this conflict, even though the issues are declared to be of a purely aesthetic nature. Westminster Council's Public Arts Committee have objected both to the position and the size of the statue. They have deemed it inappropriate to place the statue in the prominent position of the north terrace of the square and have suggested that it be placed closer to South Africa House. This is the outer perimeter of the square and not the square proper. Ian Walters (see Figure 1) has sculpted a nine-foot bronze figure with arms outstretched

Figure 1 Maquette of the Nelson Mandela statue planned for Trafalgar Square. Courtesy of the Mandela Statue Fund.

(urging his demands to be heard?). The committee, however, have opposed the statue on the grounds that they find the size and shape of the hands disagreeable. To this opposition Walters has responded by saying, 'My feeling is that the expression of the sculpture … the tension of the message and the urgency … is all in the hands. I feel that it is non-negotiable' (cited in Muir 2003).

The moment when the historically excluded is included is incredibly revealing. The unease generated by the position and posture of a black figure in a privileged public space invokes the constitutive boundaries of the imagination of the nation. The consistency of the play of national symbols, stories and monuments is jarred by the impending arrival of this figure. It threatens to dislodge the established configuration of the inter/national and history. Rather like the *awaaz* (sound/volume) in the square, noted above, this is a presence that prods us to look again at what flanks, towers above, circles and is inside and outside the production of national space. Henri Lefebvre states that monumental space operates as a means of 'separating the sacred from the profane and of repressing those gestures which are not prescribed by monumental space – in short, as a means of banishing the obscene.' (2002: 226). Perhaps Mandela's bronze hands incite a sense of unease in the committee because they signal an assured sense of anti-racism that is at odds with the rest of the figures in the square. In this context, Mandela's hands represent a discordant event, at variance with the hegemonic definition of international (imperial) leadership, as it has previously been depicted in the square.

By encroaching upon the symbolic domain of the nation, this black figure, whose proportions, postures and positioning are disputed, brings to light the racialised norm. The anticipated dissonance caused by the statue invites us to consider what is the somatic norm, and who has an undisputed right to currently pass as the universal figure of leadership. Moreover, which antinomies underlie the constitutive edges of its construction? They are gendered as well as racialised.

Enshrined in Stone

Benedict Anderson states that one of the most powerful ways in which the mythos of the nation is sustained is through monuments and ceno-taphs to the Unknown Soldier (1991: 9). These, he remarks, enable any figure in the 'imagined community' to occupy this subject position. In response, Joanne Sharp points to the gendered nature of the figure and argues, 'But surely the Unknown Soldier is not entirely anonymous. We can all be fairly sure that the soldier is not called Sarah, Lucy or Jane' (1996: 99).[2]

A group of women Members of Parliament, including Patricia Hewitt and Betty Boothroyd, have recently campaigned to place a permanent monument to the women who contributed to WW1 and WW2 on a fourth plinth in Trafalgar Square, which has stood empty for over 150 years and been the subject of countless proposals and counter-proposals for memorials. Interestingly, they have wanted to combine this with a tribute to the Queen Mother's contribution to the war effort.

So far, the plinth has been used as a rotating public space for contemporary art. In June 2001 a sculpture by the artist Rachel Whiteread featured a clear resin cast, with a hard crystalline surface, of the fourteen-foot-high granite plinth, inverted and placed on top of it. The artist invites us to pause in a quiet moment on the whole question of monumentality. The colour of the resin alters with the light of the day. Here is a monument that does not aim to solidify space to a time in the past. It could be said that national monuments and especially those of war remove 'traces of violence and death, negativity and aggressiveness in social practice' and 'replace them with a tranquil power and certitude which can encompass violence and terror'. Dissent, between classes and different groups, is absorbed and consensus is rendered 'practical and concrete'. In effect, 'the repressive element' of war and nation building is 'metamorphosed into exaltation' (Lefebvre 2002: 220–2).

That being said, the normative figure of leadership and especially in battle has been masculine. Women's inclusion into the nation has been quite specific. Certainly, ample quantities of stone have been utilised to carve female statues of the nation. In these, though, women predominantly feature as symbols of virtue, beauty, nurture and justice. Courage is a resident narrative in these monuments. Often women are feminine in the shape and gestures of their bodies alongside symbols of battle. Just around the corner from Trafalgar Square, at Admiralty Arch, for instance, a female figure cradles a sub-machine-gun in her lap. At the top of the Victoria monument on The Mall, a female figure 'spreads her huge, albatross wings over marble statues below, of the old Queen herself, surrounded by Courage, Truth and Charity' (Warner 1996: 54). There are abundant concrete adulations of women serving a metaphoric function. It is men, however, who are metonymically linked to the nation. Women feature as allegorical figures that signify the virtues of the nation. It is men who literally represent and defend the nation. It is they who are the somatic norm, when it comes to actual leadership on the ground, so to speak. This, of course, is not to say that the symbols of women as courage and protectors of the nation do not affect how others see women in leadership, as well as how they model themselves. These symbols can be a resource that they harness to hail the nation; the most obvious example of this is the symbiosis that pertained between Margaret Thatcher and the allegory of Britannia (Nunn 2002).

Shifts in Bodies/Space

There has been a notable metonymic shift in the increased presence of women and racialised minorities into spaces in the public realm which have predominantly been occupied by white men. The shift is undoubtedly slow and uneven across organisations and different sectors. There are also, of course, considerable differences between gender and 'race'. While the 'glass ceiling' has been cracked quite significantly with gender, for 'race' a 'concrete ceiling' has just been chipped ever so slightly. The cultural landscape of the public sphere has nevertheless been the site of a change that warrants close attention. Looking across space/time, in terms of gender, Doreen Massey notes:

> I can remember very clearly a sight which often used to strike me when I was nine or ten years old. I lived then on the outskirts of Manchester, and 'Going into Town' was a relatively big occasion; it took over half an hour and we went on the top deck of a bus. On the way into town we would cross the wide shallow valley of the River Mersey, and my memory is of dank, muddy fields spreading away into a cold, misty distance. And all of it – all of these acres of Manchester – was divided up into football pitches and rugby pitches. And on Saturdays, which was when we went into Town, the whole vast area would be covered with hundreds of little people, all running around after balls, as far as the eye could see. (It seemed from the top of the bus like a vast, animated Lowry painting, with all the little people in rather brighter colours than Lowry used to paint them, and with cold red legs.)
>
> I remember all this very sharply. And I remember, too, it striking me very clearly – even as a puzzled, slightly thoughtful little girl – that all this huge stretch of the Mersey flood plain had been entirely given over to boys.
>
> I did not go to those playing fields – they seemed barred, another world (though today, with more nerve and some consciousness of being a space-invader, I do stand on football terraces – and love it). (Massey 1996:185)

The sheer maleness of particular public spaces and women's experience of increasingly occupying them while still being conscious of being 'space invaders' even while they enjoy these places is vividly captured by Massey. To this, of course, we could add that the sheer whiteness of spaces is also being altered, that is, on the football terraces, as well as elsewhere, in a wider sense. To be of and in a space, while at the same time not quite belonging to it, is pertinent to Massey's positionality.

Formally, today, women and racialised minorities can enter positions that they were previously excluded from. And the fact that they do is evidence of this. However, social spaces are not blank and open for any body to occupy. There is a connection between bodies and space, which is built, repeated and contested over time. While all can, in theory, enter, it is certain types of bodies that are tacitly designated as being the 'natural' occupants of specific positions. Some bodies are deemed as having the right to belong, while others are marked out as trespassers, who are, in accordance with how both spaces and bodies are imagined (politically, historically and conceptually), circumscribed as being 'out of place'. Not being the somatic norm, they are space invaders. The coupling of particular spaces with specific types of bodies is no doubt subject to change; this usually, however, is not without consequence as it often breaks with how bodies have been placed.

The presence of women and racialised minorities continues to locate what are now insiders as outsiders. Being both insiders and outsiders, they occupy a tenuous location. Not being the somatic norm, they don't have an undisputed right to occupy this space. Yet they are still insiders. Their arrival brings into clear relief what has been able to pass as the invisible, unmarked and undeclared somatic norm. These new bodies highlight the constitutive boundaries of who can pass as the universal human, and hence who can be the ideal figure of leadership. What has been constructed out in the historical and conceptual imagination is brought to the fore.

Research on the Universal Somatic Norm

There has been an in-depth and extended level of theoretical discussion regarding the very particular embodied subject that has been able to masquerade as the universal. There has, however, been an extraordinary lack of engagement with the theoretical material by those who conduct more substantive research. The impact of the conceptual and historical imagination of the universal somatic norm upon the everyday location of women and racialised minorities in institutions has not been granted the attention it deserves.

There has been a propensity to undertake analysis of 'race', stratification and employment by looking at segregation patterns in terms of numbers and monitoring procedures. The numbers are not taken as a starting-point that requires further in-depth interrogation of the terms of existence. Any form of cultural analysis at best concerns itself with religious practices, food and drink or language, and much of it is still, unfortunately, of the old static, essentialist, culturalist model (Lawrence 1982; Gilroy 1993). After the murder of the black teenager Steven Lawrence and the ensuing MacPherson Report (MacPherson of Cluny 1999), as well as the Race Relations Amendment Act (2000), there has been a significant level of public discussion of institutional racism. However, the obsession remains with changing organisations (diversifying them) by getting more racialised bodies into organisations. How institutional racism operates in extremely subtle ways, most especially through the designation of the somatic norm, remains unexplored.

The area of gender, work and organisations has, in contrast, developed a broad array of theoretical and methodological tools for understanding gender in complex ways. The work on unions, managers and the financial sector has been exemplary in this regard (Cockburn 1987, 1991; Hearn and Parkin 1987; Roper 1993; Collinson and Hearn 1996; Itzin and Newman 1996; Crompton 1997; McDowell 1997). However, while the masculine norm as a force in the workplace is an implicit consideration in this field, it lacks explicit attention. Most of these studies have not fully engaged with the sophisticated debates on gender and political theory. Hence the force of the somatic norm remains under-theorised.

The political theorists themselves have not yet managed to successfully marry complicated feminist theory with substantive research. This is partly explained by the fact that they operate on the plane of 'pure' theory. And the political scientists who do conduct research on women in political organisations, by looking at femocrats or women in Parliament, have, largely in response to the doxa that prevails in their field, employed overly quantitative methods of analysis (Lovenduski and Norris 1995; Childs 2001). This approach, even if it is informed by qualitative data, does not easily lend itself to complex theoretical issues.[3] These researchers are no doubt aware of theoretical debates on the universal figure of leadership, yet the impact of this upon the everyday life of men and women in politics is not integrated with their research.

While 'race' is a significant part of theoretical debates on difference in feminist political theory, it does not feature in any serious way in the area of either women and politics or gender, work and organisations. And, when it does, it is usually seen to reside in minority ethnic women. Thus they become the focus of attention while 'race' is ex-nominated from white bodies, male and female. Thus the relative degree to which white women are the somatic norm, on the grounds of whiteness, gets overlooked. The extent to which their whiteness grants them a certain level of 'ontological complicity' (c.f. Bourdieu 1990b: 11–12) with normative institutional cultures, even while they are, on the grounds of gender and possibly class, 'space invaders', remains hidden.

As Matter Out of Place

As matter out of place, the presence of women and racialised minorities institutes a whole series of processes which signal that they are 'space invaders'. While undertaking an in-depth account of these processes, it is important to underline the differences between 'race' and gender. An analysis that is appropriate for one must not be automatically moved across to the other. Differences between occupational fields must also not be homogenised and collapsed into each other. At the same time, though, in between the differences of professions there is room for a kaleidoscopic framework of analysis. The analytical framework developed in this book could certainly be extended to sites which have not been paid attention. The processes identified are, in different configurations, encountered by 'space invaders' in institutions across the board. Each assemblage points to the impact of the universal somatic norm as a force that situates women and racialised minorities in a tenuous position of being both insiders and outsiders who are, to varying degrees, rhetorically speaking 'space invaders'.

The observation of more or less different bodies statistically, in terms of 'race' or gender, in the predominantly white and male echelons of power does not by itself speak of the contradictory terms of their existence or, indeed, how their presence is received in an overwhelmingly white or male outfit. It fails to appreciate the complexity of coexisting in organisations and élite positions previously reserved for specific types of bodies. In contrast, a consideration of the terms of coexistence allows us to see how less obvious and more nuanced exclusion operates within institutions via the tacit reservation of privileged positions for the somatic norm.

In a discussion 'Of Men and Empire', Chapter 2 addresses the historical and theoretical construction of the political subject. An instance of ontological anxiety faced by Winston Churchill helps to unfurl the series of distinctions and boundaries underlying the construction of the ideal political somatic norm. Demarcations of masculine and feminine bodies and the concomitant public and private domain point to how women in the privileged spaces of the political realm are matter out of place. These boundaries are complicated further by looking at how 'race' and colonialism have been central to the formation of (imperial) public masculinity and femininity. Gendered constructions of national boundaries and differences between women have contributed to how Europe's constitutive outside has figured in the making of political and private/public realms. The ontological sense of importance afforded to the master masculine political subject, on the basis of these foundations, is, as shown by this chapter, built on a tenuous set of boundaries that are constantly under risk. The repressed or denied body in the realm of reason all too easily erupts into visibility when the hitherto excluded arrive on the scene.

Chapter 3 turns to the encounter when dissonant bodies take up space in positions that have not been 'reserved' for them. Their presence defies long-standing boundaries. Witnessing this socio-spatial impact, two fundamental processes are observed – disorientation and amplification. A muted sense of terror and threat underlies the reception of racialised minorities and women in predominantly white and masculine domains. 'Known' through a limited set of framings, these bodies jar and destabilise an exclusive sense of place. As the 'unknown', who defy conventions and boundaries, they represent the potentially monstrous, whose somatic arrival invades the social and psychic. The 'organisational terror' they are seen to pose is exacerbated by an increase in the numbers of 'black' and female bodies in privileged positions, as well by any informal or formal support groups they might set up or join.

Processes of in/visibility are discussed as an aspect of the designation of '(In)Visible Universal Bodies' in Chapter 4. The privilege of being racially unmarked is identified as a crucial condition of being a universal figure of leadership. Those who are conversely ethnically marked are particularised as representatives of specific interests. Seen in confined terms that lock the body with a set of ideas, they are unseen as the more general representatives of universal concerns. Not being the ideal occupants of privileged positions, 'space invaders' endure a burden of doubt, a burden of representation, infantilisation and super-surveillance. Existing under the optic lens of suspicion and surveillance, racialised bodies in politics, the arts, universities and bureaucracies are all too easily seen to be lacking the desired competencies.

Chapter 5 takes an in-depth look at the contradictions faced by women when they enter male outfits deemed to be ill-fitting. Conflicting occupational and gendered scripts make the performative enactment of positions highly problematic. The chapter focuses on the way in which masculinities are performatively ritualised in the House of Commons. What happens to female bodies when they enter this aggressive, territorial and fraternal political theatre is documented through interview accounts with women MPs. The latter part of this chapter considers how women MPs stylise femininities in a male outfit. Margaret Thatcher, still the most famous script of a woman in politics in the UK, is granted specific attention. The combination of exaggerated forms of femininity and masculinity, as well as imperial militaristic splendour, was her hallmark. Thus a male outfit was fashioned anew within the confines of existing gendered performative directives.

The centrality of specific types of bodily hexis to recruitment to the upper echelons of institutions is never explicitly stated. Instead, they operate as tacit criteria. Chapter 6 introduces the notion of imperial/legitimate language in order to shed light on how civility is measured via the body and most especially through how the body speaks and interacts. The metamorphic quality of imperial/legitimate language enables racialised minorities to become human, in the full sense. They are the bodies that are more likely to be respected and accepted in institutions. In fact, in some cases, treated as rare entities, they are overly praised. Thus those who do not conform to this norm will find it difficult to be heard. However, those who do 'fit' in terms of bodily hexis are never completely assimilated. In some senses, their presence as racialised bodies disrupts the somatic norm. They represent a menace, even though they fail to displace the centrifugal force of the somatic norm.

It is commonplace to speak of particular groups being marginal in respect of outsiders to particular privileged positions. Despite the fact that talk of intersections has become *de rigueur*, there is a reluctance to discuss how outsiders are simultaneously insiders. Chapter 7 complicates the positionality of 'space invaders' by looking at how they become insiders. It considers how all staff concur in the chequer-board terrain of hierarchies and social cloning. They have an investment in their professions. More importantly, they have advocates and sponsors whose endorsements are crucial. And to varying degrees they know how to operate in the field. Some, due to their social trajectories and habitus, move with ease and cadence. Throwing light on intersections of race, gender and class, ontological complicity is identified as the substance of differentiated inclusion.

Ontological denial of embodiment is implicit in institutional narratives of professionalism. The final part of Chapter 7 addresses the tortuous journey of naming 'race' and gender. As renegade acts, they invite suspicion, especially when they are enacted by those who already don't quite fit.

–2–

Of Men and Empire

I find a woman's intrusion into the House of Commons as embarrassing as if she burst into my bathroom when I had nothing with which to defend myself, not even a sponge.

Winston Churchill, cited in Vallance, *Women in the House*

I'm interested in that condition that seems to be abidingly static and at the same time dynamic ... I'm interested to frame that effect: it's the effect of an enormous weight ... out of balance. An apparently out of balance form.

Anish Kapoor, cited in Tazzi, Bhabha and Kapoor,
Anish Kapoor

For Winston Churchill, that often quoted man of 'wise' words,[1] the arrival of the first woman MP in the House of Commons (Nancy Astor), for a split second, brings on a state of disorientation and ontological anxiety. Bodies, intimate space, privacy, territoriality, boundaries and threat are all features of his response. His sense of self and the deep intimacy he has with the political space he is standing in are, for a moment, put out of balance. This individual encounter is embedded in a series of wider socio-political encounters central to the making of privileged positions in the public sphere and especially the body politic as a masculine domain of whiteness.

The concomitant reliance on gendered boundaries alongside the imagination of far-off landscapes has made race and gender central to who is defined as human enough to be the ideal political 'individual'. This chapter will consider the set of oppositions that have produced the embodied specificity of the disembodied political 'individual'. We shall see that there is a somatic norm whose contours are undeclared and firmly entrenched in space and time, even while the tenuous nature of these boundaries is constantly under risk of eruption.

Bodily Boundaries

The fragility of the masculine claim to public space and most specifically the body politic is disturbed by the arrival of the abject. That is, the advent of what the place of rationality, reason, culture and debate has sought to take transcendence from – the feminine (nature, emotion and the bodily) – incites a sense of unease.

The stability of the identity of the body politic is constituted through a series of oppositional binaries (borders) which define it in contradistinction to the feminine/private and all that it is beheld as representing. Historically the political/public realm has been 'constructed through the exclusion of women and all that we symbolize' (Pateman 1995: 52). Thus the presence of the feminine as a bodily entity disrupts the partition between the private and the public even if it does not render it altogether invalid. As the ways we live in space affect our 'corporeal alignments, comportment, and orientations' (Grosz 1999: 385), a female body in a male dwelling, as the abject (Kristeva 1980), threatens corporeal and psychic boundaries and, in the case before us, brings on a state of disorientation.

Churchill speaks of the arrival of a woman in a male space as an intrusion of a bodily kind. He feels naked, somehow exposed and vulnerable. His body is revealed as being important to how he orients himself, and yet the body is denied in somatophobic political discourse. Even though metaphors of the body have served to naturalise political forms, the universal political individual is declared to be disembodied. Neutrality and transcendence of the bodily by the mind are what are declared as the norm. Discussions of the political realm, radical or conservative, imagine an 'image of the polity [which] is anthropomorphic' (Gatens 1996: 23). The sexual subtext is not mentioned in the mass of malestream political theory. Gender-blindness has been the orthodoxy in political theory, even in radical critiques of liberal democracy.

The morphological dimensions of this fraudulent fantasy have been fully documented by feminist political theorists (Ortner 1974; Okin 1992; Nelson 1996). Speaking of the body in the work of the grandfathers of parliamentary representation, especially Hobbes, Locke and Rousseau, Elizabeth Grosz lays the masquerade to rest when she smokes out the gendered attributes of the body politic:

> The state parallels the body; artifice mirrors nature. The correspondence between the body and the body politic is more or less exact and codified: the King usually represents the Head of the State; the populace is usually

represented as the body. The law has been compared to the body's nerves; the military to its arms, commerce to its legs or stomach, and so on. The exact correspondences vary from text to text. However, if there is a morphological correspondence between the artificial commonwealth (the Leviathan) and the human body in this pervasive metaphor of the body politic, the body is rarely attributed a sex. What, one might ask, takes on the metaphoric function of the genitals in the body politic? What kind of genitals are they? Does the body politic have a sex? (Grosz 1995: 106)

The neutered neutral body is found wanting as a masculine (no)body which by no means includes every(body). The civil body is 'fashioned after only one of the two bodies of humankind' (Pateman 1995: 34). An isomorphic relationship is located between the male body, Western thought (philosophy) and society (polis). But this is not an isomorphism which is, as Grosz warns us, a 'mirroring of nature in artifice' (1999: 385); it is an unmediated or direct relation not to the male body but rather to imaginary and symbolic representations. Thus the 'modern body politic is based on an image of a masculine body which reflects fantasies about the value and capacities of that body' (Gatens 1996: 25).

Public/Private

The undeclared masculine norm in 'conventional political thought has offered us men in a gender-free guise', while 'all talk of universal rights or citizenship or rules has taken one sex alone as the standard, leaving the other one out in the cold' (Phillips 1993: 62). Illustrating the connection between the creation of the public sphere, enlightenment thought and women's exclusion, Joan Landes says: 'the gendered organization of nature, truth, and opinion [has meant that] women's (legal and con-stitutional) exclusion from the public sphere was a constitutive, not a marginal or accidental feature of the bourgeois public from the start' (1998: 143).

Pateman historicises how women were left 'out in the cold' in the making of citizenship. She states that contract law was certainly radical to the extent that it defeated patriarchal political power (the rule of kings over sons) on the basis of the principle that sons were born free and equal and that political authority and obligation were conventional. She draws our attention to the sexual contract implicit in the social contract of equality and liberty. The social contract was a masculine fraternal pact. Theorists of the state have, however, repressed this side of the social contract. Whilst sons were freed from patriarchs (the law of fathers) to form fraternities, women were still subject to the sexual or conjugal aspect of patriarchy. This exclusion leads to a public realm and a notion of equality that 'is fashioned after the image of the male "individual"', who is constituted 'through the separation of civil society from women' (Pateman 1995: 46). Significantly, the separation is itself constructed on the basis of a patriarchal separation of the sexes. Pateman stresses that sexual difference and the subordination of women in the private sphere are absolutely central to the formation of the social contract. She says:

> the meanings of 'private' and 'public' are mutually interdependent: the 'public' cannot be comprehended in isolation. Properly to understand the conception of a public world and the capacities and characteristics that are required to participate within it demands, at the same time, an understanding of what is excluded from the public and why the exclusion takes place. The 'public' rests on a particular conception of the 'private' and vice versa. (1995: 3)

The dichotomy between nature and truth is implicitly mapped on to a separation of masculine and feminine domains and bodies. One of the major fantasies of the male body is that the finest minds are able to overcome the limits of the body, which is after all framed as an obstacle to pure rational thought. There is a masculinist denial of the male body while women are over-determined by the materiality of their bodies. Thus 'certain disembodied masculine selves emerge as central at the expense of the materiality of others' (Probyn 1993: 60). Logic and rationality are symbolically male and women are outside them. Women are their bodies, but men are not, and women are therefore destined to inferiority in all spheres requiring rationality.

The separation of the mind and body, reason and nature, is absorbed in the public realm to the extent that there is repulsion and even fear of the body. Hence the body is treated with suspicion, as a site of unruly passions and appetite that might disrupt the pursuit of truth and knowledge. There is an association of the body with gross physicality. The 'separation of civil society from the familial sphere is thus also a division between men's reason and women's bodies' (Pateman 1995: 45). In this sense men take flight in civil society away from the familial and the feminine, even while the family/women nourish them. Woman is a place, that is, as Luce Irigaray puts it, 'from whence the "subject" continues to draw his reserves, his re-sources, yet [is] unable to recognise them/her' (cited in Whitford 1991: 53). Hers is an unacknowledged contribution. Woman is a place – a container, an envelope – through which man marks the limits of his identity.

Ontological Anxiety: Churchill, Kapoor and Irigaray

Irigaray argues that fantasies of the capacities of public man are reflected all around him, in language, in laws, in dwellings and in emotions. Each of these work together to form what she refers to as a 'palace of mirrors' (1985a: 137). She adds that the mirrors are flat, and that the flat mirror 'privileges the relation of man to his fellow man' (1985b: 154). Viewing Churchill's scene from this perspective, it is possible to argue that he was literally surrounded by halls of mirrors in Westminster, where hand-painted, soft-focused portraits of the great and the good (men), in grand gold-embossed frames, flank the walls. These images tower over corridors of power where the male simulacrum is repeated back to itself, as confirmation of who men are and what they are.

The 'coherence' of the mirrors is assured 'so long as they remain uninterrupted' (Irigaray 1985b: 75). In Churchill's encounter they became interrupted by the presence of a female body in this masculine domain (House). The interruption induced a mild case of ontological anxiety. An ontological disruption of the subject questions what the subject is. The whole basis of an identity which had relied on a border is placed at stake when the boundaries do not obey the slicing of mind/body, man/woman. With the body coded as female *per se*, women's bodies represent foreign matter that threatens to contaminate the realm of serene, clean thought. The fear of fusion, of the boundaries bleeding into each other, drains ideal political man (in this case Churchill) of the strength he derives from the separation.

The invisibility of the disembodied male body becomes visible, as he in this fleeting moment is deprived of his armour of culture and reason and stands naked with, as he puts it, 'nothing with which to defend myself'. In the normal state of play, the subject is invisible to himself as he looks out from his 'palace of mirrors' and contemplates the world (Irigaray 1985a: 212–13). Now, for Churchill, his contemplation is reduced to that most private of places, the bathroom, used as a simile for the House of Commons. Although he has seen reflections of himself in the mirrors, symbolic and literal, all around him, the corporeality of the male form has been denied in fantastic projections. In this encounter, what he refers to as an 'intrusion' has laid his body bare.

In a moment of disorientation, Churchill alerts us to the pyschosomatic dimensions of public masculinity. The demarcation of an inside/outside around the body, of the body as a territory with a line 'drawn around it' (Irigaray 1992: 17), is for a remote second turned upside down by the movement of the outside into the inside. The bounded and tight skin that is assigned to him, who has made the House *his* and has positioned *her* outside it, is threatened by an intimate proximity, whose elasticity exceeds the defining limits of body/space to the point of engulfing them.

If it 'is our positioning within space, both as the point of perspectival access to space, and also an object for others in space, that gives the subject a coherent identity and ability to manipulate things, including its own body parts, in space' (Grosz 1995: 92), could it be that Churchill's positioning of himself in the public sphere and its (disembodied) bodily characterisations in relation to the private was momentarily toppled? The traditional sources of his historical and conceptual schema entered the category of being at risk. Hence he is disorientated. The work of the artist Anish Kapoor can be particularly fruitful for thinking about this encounter.

By 'dwelling in doubt' (Kapoor, cited in Tazzi *et al.* 1998: 38) as a place of productivity, Kapoor's art hangs on to a state of transitionality. Where time and space develop their own 'affects – anxiety, unease, restlessness' (Bhabha 1998: 16). The connectivity of our psychological states of mind with our bodies can't be avoided in the practice of viewing/ experiencing his sculptures. His sculptures draw in the eye as well as the body, provoking feelings of disorientation or dislocation. Disorientation and the consequent reorientation are, for Kapoor, productive moments, where change can occur. They invite one to pause and to reconsider one's place in space. This is precisely why Kapoor tries to slow time down and make that moment of pause as long as possible. What is vital to his work is reverie, a moment of loss. The sculptures manipulate the viewers into thinking about their presence in time and space. Standing in front of the installations, the viewer is confronted with a distinct, immediate reality. Kapoor seeks to bring out what he refers to as the 'resident narrative' (cited in Tazzi *et al.* 1998: 27). Or, as Pier Luigi Tazzi puts it, the work offers us 'refractions that give substance to the blind vision inside' (1998: 105).

In a series of installations which make use of reflective surfaces in highly polished aluminium and steel spherical sculptures, a piece titled *Turning the World Inside Out* (see the image on the front cover of this book) is of a globe-shaped sculpture with a receding, concave centre. In the mirror surface of the work, spectator and architecture merge in a distorted and yet alluring reflected image. The reflective surfaces appear to engulf the viewer and the surrounding space. Commenting on a piece in this series, Homi Bhabha observes: 'interiority and exteriority fail to preserve their determining dimensions. If the mirror sucks in, it also spits out – it reflects and refluxes. Such a reading illustrates the motility embodied in the reflective surface of the mirror and exemplifies those non-physical things, the intellectual things, the possibilities that are available *through* the material' (Bhabha 1998: 25).

If we keep in mind that, for Irigaray, woman is man's *'projective map* for the purposes of guaranteeing the totality of the system – the excess factor' (1985b: 108) and we take what has been said of Kapoor's sculptures and revisit the material scene of Churchill, then it is possible to see that, when the excess factor erupts from her projected place and no longer guarantees the totality of the system, it could be that she has the potential to be not a flat mirror but one with spherical surfaces: one that 'reassembles' both 'walls and faces' in the Commons, with 'surfaces that blur together' so that 'interiority' and 'exteriority' do not maintain their dimensions. The female refracts the play of the fantasy of oppositions. And hence we have ontological anxiety.

Whether Churchill can take the 'refluxes' in what 'reflects' back to him when a woman MP arrives in a public dwelling that is simultaneously an ever so private space for certain types of masculinity is another question. Dwelling in doubt is a state that is not easily taken up by masculine, imperial, sovereign, political subjects who have developed an assured sense of ontological importance. This is an identity made through identification with knowledge and sovereignty of the world, while others are dis-identified with this place. It is based on a 'political model of a single leader, judged the best, and the only one capable of governing more or less civil citizens possessed of a more or less human identity' (Irigaray 2000:122).

In order to fully grasp masculinities (Chapman and Rutherford 1988; Hearn 1992; Collinson and Hearn 1996; Mac and Ghaill 1996; Segal 1997) and the types of fraternal relations which dwell in the public realm, a global perspective is required. And, to keep the notion of women's exclusion in historical context, we need to always bear in mind that: 'At different times, different kinds of beings have been excluded from the pact, often simply by virtue of their corporeal specificity. Slaves, foreigners, women, the conquered, children, the working classes have all been excluded from political participation, at one time or another, by their bodily specificity' (Gatens 1996: 23).

The Racialised Sovereign

> They are two coextensive and complementary faces of one development: rule within Europe and European rule over the world.
>
> Hardt and Negri, *Empire*

Drawing attention to the contradictory aspect of modernity and enlighten-ment, Hardt and Negri (2000) argue that science, knowledge and demo-cracy were reactionary as well as revolutionary. These developments consisted of a storm of theoretical acts that were immensely creative and open. The tumultuous concoction also included the forces of control and the quest for order.[2] And ultimately a renaissance of ideas was overcome by the energies of domination. What Hardt and Negri highlight in the above quote is the close relationship between the emergence of domination and sovereignty over here (in Europe) and over there (the colonised world). In *Between Camps*, Paul Gilroy (2000: 65) similarly states that rationality, enlightenment and universal humanity were extremely liberating and revolutionary. At the same time, though, he stresses that, because rationality colluded with the irrationalism of the racial sciences (what he terms 'raciology'), 'enlightenment pretensions toward universality were punctured from the moment of their conception in the womb of the colonial space. Their very foundations were de-stabilized by their initial exclusionary configuration.'[3]

Although colonial 'adventures' and rule in the empire have been key to how the political realm has been conceived in Europe, this aspect of sovereignty, like the sexual contract, is repressed. Charles Mills locates the discipline of political philosophy as being 'that unfortunate area of backwardness'. He criticises this field of the academy for, on the one hand, 'tacitly taking the white body as normative' (1998: 120) and, on the other hand, denying the racial nature of the polity. Just as feminists have criticised political theorists for overlooking and concealing the masculine image upon which the body politic and hypothetical debates of the body politic are based, he states that scholars have been reluctant to consider the racial exclusions which underpin notions of humanity, democracy and the political subject. In his book *The Racial Contract* (1997), he takes inspiration from Pateman's analysis of the repressed sexual contract to develop the notion of the repressed racial contract. He argues that the social contract has simultaneously been fraternal and racial (white). Interestingly Mills and Pateman are now working on a project that brings their long-standing separate projects on the racial and sexual contract together. This is a necessary task, after all:[4] 'If you look at the famous texts, and the political developments of empires and the world-wide system of states, you can see that the original contract had at least three interrelated dimensions: (1) the social contract, which of course is the standard one that everyone is taught, (2) the sexual contract, and (3) the racial contract' (Pateman and Puwar 2002: 126).

In a similar vein to feminists who have argued that the exclusion of women from the social contract was not an exception or an accident but was absolutely pivotal to the fraternal contract, Mills states that the racial contract was not a 'deviation' or an 'afterthought' but rather it was the norm. Race was a 'central shaping constituent' of Western enlightenment ideals (1997: 14) and from its actual genesis 'the polity was in fact a racial one' (1997: 57). Locating his claim historically he explains that the:

> golden age of contract theory (1650–1800) overlapped with the growth of a European capitalism whose development was stimulated by the voyages of exploration that increasingly gave the contract a racial subtext. The evolution of the modern version of the contract, characterised by an antipatriarchalist Enlightenment liberalism, with its proclamations of the equal rights, autonomy, and freedom for all men, thus took place simultaneously with the massacre, expropriation, and subjection to hereditary slavery of men at least apparently human. This contradiction needs to be reconciled; it is reconciled through the Racial Contract, which essentially denies their personhood and restricts the terms of the social contract to whites ... The Racial Contract is thus the truth of the social contract. (1997: 64)

The colonial project racialised personhood. Just as discourses constituted the female body as an unsuitable occupant of the body politic, certain racialised bodies were also deemed unsuitable participants of the politic. Mills writes, 'the Racial Contract is explicitly predicated on a politics of the body which is related to the body politic through restrictions on which bodies are "politic". There are bodies impolitic whose owners are judged incapable of forming or fully entering into a body politic' (1997: 53).

Within the European imperialist project space was normed on three different levels: macro (countries and continents), local (cities and neighbourhoods) and micro (bodies). 'The Racial Contract norms (and races) space, demarcating civil and wild spaces' (Mills 1997: 41). Black bodies are represented as coming from uncivilised spaces, wildernesses where people are savages and need taming. In this racially dichotomous hierarchy, whites[5] are associated with spirit and mind, the flight from the body. In contrast, blacks are associated with nature and the body. In the racial classificatory schema, it is only white Europeans, because they are designated to be fully human, 'lords of humankind', who are seen to have the right personal constitution to reside in political constitutions. Blacks, in negation, are defined as humanoids who are not human enough to reside in the body politic. Mills emphasises that non-white persons are categorised in a manner that 'morally, epistemically and aesthetically' establishes their 'ontological inferiority' (1997: 118). Positions of leadership and authority are considered to be beyond their ontological status.

Written on the back of European declarations of sovereignty sat the colonised in a superior estimation of where Europe located itself in comparison with populations in other continents. Inhabited by 'noble savages', their level of 'maturity' was not quite a match to the white European, classed man. Moreover, his laws and polities were created in a bid to take transcendence from the 'state of nature' as optimised in racialised non-European spaces as well as in the feminised space of the private sphere. Placed in a timeless zone before 'contract', the colonies were differentiated from the colonising state by their affinity with nature and a lack of reason.

States of nature in the social and political thought of the grandfathers of democracy are featured in distant lands. Hobbes classified American Indians in the 'New World' as 'Indians' in the 'woods of America' (Goldberg 2002: 40–4). Locke classified the Hottentots of Cape Town as Africa's negroes, who, like the American Indians, were infantile. While Locke thought they could be civilised and thus be historically lifted out of this state, for Rousseau their fate was biologically given. As far as Rousseau was concerned, noble savages could even become Christians but they could not be civilised. John Stuart Mill's masterly texts on liberalism were written out of British policies in India. He worked for the East India Company and sought to make British democracy compatible with despotic rule in India (Parekh 1995). For India, Mill subscribed to an ambivalent and what Bhabha sees as being a potentially unstable position of being 'father and oppressor' in addressing the 'ruled and reviled'. In this equation, democracy (peace and progress) was doubled as 'vigorous despotism' (Bhabha 1994: 97).

Across time Charles Mills identifies two types of racial contract: the first type existed during the epochs of European conquest, African slavery and European colonialism. In this period, blacks were excluded from the polity through a formal system of juridical white supremacy. In the present period, we are living with the second type of racial contract, whereby the racial contract has written itself out of formal existence. This means that the terms of the social contract have been formally extended to apply to everyone, so that 'persons' is no longer coextensive with 'whites'. In these conditions, white supremacy is no longer constitutionally and juridically enshrined, but is rather a matter of social, political, cultural and economic privilege, based on a legacy of colonial conquest. Just as the legacy of the sexual contract continues to have ramifications for the social position of women, long after the formal inclusion of women in the social contract, similarly the legacy of the racial contract continues in an informal sense. Mills argues that, within the terms of the second type of racial contract, exclusion of black people is no longer explicit and formally endorsed. Instead, it is much more 'latent' (1997: 75) and slippery to recognise and name.

A Gendered/Racialised Affair

The encounter with new places of conquest was never purely a racialised affair; rather, it was replete with gendered distinctions. In the making of national and international fraternities, hierarchies of inclusion were wrapped up with each other, whereby the global overlapped with gender and vice versa. The racial contract has been important to the way in which racial relations and the creation of political and philosophical thought within the ambit of imperialism became mediated and imagined in the fantasies of European man as leader and thinker. Overlaid by a sexual contract, as well as one of class, the European knight in shining armour trampled here and there seeking out savagery and exotica while acquiring spices, gold, tea, sugar, cloth, jewels and land along the way. Intrinsic to the project of despotic democracy has been the 'saving' of women from other places. In Spivak's words, this is the project of 'White men saving brown women from brown men' (1988a: 296), making way for what Sunder Rajan describes as a 'trope of chivalry', a rite of passage for young white men into amorous masculinity (1993: 6).

It was not, however, just the knight in shining armour who set about saving women in the colonies under the masquerade of the 'rescue paradigm' (Sunder Rajan 1993: 6). Western women, 'imperial ladies', also donned this cloak, albeit with a different affectation, to style, perhaps unconsciously, a political position and identity for themselves (Chaudhuri and Strobel 1992; Burton 1994). In the face of conceptions of the liberal political 'individual' that did not include women proper, but in a differentiated way, they could use charitable postures which maintained distinctions between 'us' and 'them' to measure and judge the lives of 'Other' women through a 'yardstick' that took the lives of middle-class women in the West as the norm, 'as the implicit referent' (Mohanty 1988: 64) to assert themselves as agents against the exclusionary political agendas of white masculinity. The fashioning of Western women as enlightened agents who took on the mission of relieving the patriarchal plight of women in the colonies was pivotal to the yielding of political rights and agency by Western women. Thus 'in the process of campaigning for women whom they considered to be more badly treated than themselves... Western women could achieve a subject position for themselves, often at the expense of indigenous women's subject position and sense of agency' (Mills, S. 1998: 105).

Here we see how it is too simple a story to say that women are simply excluded from the state. Instead, through a set of hierarchies of inclusion they become included differently.

Private/Public

To say that women and other groups were excluded from the very conception and constitution of citizenship and the public realm should not be taken to imply that women have been altogether absent from the public realm. It is, however, more appropriate to say that their presence has been constrained by the marking of domains as masculine or feminine. In the public realm, their presence has been smothered by the definition of that space by hegemonic masculinities. Furthermore, not being the 'natural' or dominantly situated occupants of public space, under surveilling eyes their presence can be easily viewed as circumspect and untoward. Linda McDowell pays attention to the emergence of city life in nineteenth-century England and notes that:

> The very act of their appearance on the streets left the status of women open to interpretation and, often, to unwanted sexual attentions. In late Victorian Cambridge, for example, the early women students were required to wear gloves and hats when they ventured out into the public in an attempt to distinguish them from the many women of 'easy virtue' in the city. (1996: 154)

Despite the obstructions, women often overstepped the mark and moved in domains and places that sought to limit their movement but which they defined anew (Wilson 1992).[6] However liberating this process may have been, they nevertheless had to vie with respectable notions of femininity. Women from specific classes went into the private space of other women, such as working-class women or the colonies, to do public service; to fashion a place for themselves in the public realm: one that was different from that of the men, but at the same time adhered to notions of respectable femininity. Other, working-class, women were already in the less privileged public realm (Glucksman 2000). Their rhythms, however, did not and still do not dominate the space. The City, for instance, is seen to be a place of bankers and financiers while the labour of those who maintain the infrastructure of the buildings in the early hours of the morning is erased (discussed in Allen 2003: 164).

Given that women are not a homogeneous entity, within the abstract category of 'women' bodily specificities are further differentiated through a myriad set of power relations, which produce competing and hegemonic femininities. A whole series of identifications and dis-identifications between women have had an impact upon how citizenship is forged. The positioning of women in relation to each other also complicates where and how the boundary between the public and private is drawn. For the black maid, for instance, the private space of the white woman was her public space. This was her work space, where she was assessed and judged. Thus, the private dressing-room of the lady of the house operates as a public space for domestic servants (McClintock 1995).

In a mocking and patronising painting (see Figure 2), the lady of the house fashions her own identity in contradistinction to the body of her black maid. The servant is ridiculed and made to look stupid when she is dressed in her mistress's clothes. The mistress is, in the same instance,

Figure 2 A photograph taken in 1900 from a collection by Michael Graham-Stewart, a dealer in the art of Africa and the Pacific, archived at the National Maritime Museum in Greenwich (London).

illuminated for her beauty. Her maid is unable to mimic or match up to the racialised somatic norm of ideal (white) femininity. And the mistress invites the audience, to share this look (mockery), just as the maid's face is literally held up by the mistress to the mirror, for her to see her own lack. A series of dis-identifications that take place in the private place of the white woman are then framed for public viewing, in a gold-embossed frame. This image was so popular that it underwent several reproductions.

Symbols of the National

While women's bodies have been expelled from the public realm, as being contrary to the place of reason, on another level, as noted very briefly in Chapter 1, their bodies commonly feature in allegories of the nation. Images of women as being symbolically representative of the nation appear on monuments, money, anthems and warships, for instance. So, although women are not imagined as having the so-called universal and impersonal characteristics of political leadership, the virtues of the national land are mapped on to their bodies. The authenticity of the nation is seen to reside in the body of the nation, for instance the 'English rose'. The inclusion of the women into the nation is such that 'women are subsumed symbolically into the national body politic as its boundary and metaphoric limit' (McClintock 1995: 354).

Women are assigned a different relationship to the nation, one that buys into the separation of the civil and the familial, the public and the private or nature and reason, by allocating them a place in the civil domain as figurines of the familial and of nature. While somatophobia reigns over the generic, undeclared male individual of politics, the somatics of the nation assail the image of woman as the carer and onlooker of her (national as well as personal) kith and kin – the strong mother of the nation: courageous protectors and carers of the nation. Women are granted recognition within the confines of a femininity that is allied with mother-hood, land and justice.

Brought into existence as symbols of national beauty, virtue and liberty, the paradox is that, as pointed out by Marina Warner in *Monuments and Maidens* (1996), while women represent justice – for example, the Old Bailey and the Statue of Liberty – they are not seen as being capable of actually administering justice. While women serve a metaphoric function, it is men who are metonymically linked to the nation. Hence there is a huge discrepancy between the position of women in leadership roles and the symbolic images of them. All over Paris, for instance, there are grand statues of women in battle and in courageous/virtuous postures (see Warner 1996), and yet the numbers of women in élite positions in the legislature, the executive or the armed forces have lagged behind those in the rest of the world.

Within different forms of nationalism, the land of the nation is itself visualised in a female form that is beautiful, plentiful and worth dying for (Parker *et al.* 1992; Nash 1994; Yuval-Davis 1997). The right to defend the nation through armed struggle is automatically granted to men, and one which women have had to fight for. Women's bodies act as a border between nations but it is men who normatively defend this border in combat. So often territories are defended in a sexual language; the rape of women becomes the absolute assault on national land and character (Mookherjee 2003).

The production of women's bodies as national symbols was inflected by the distinction between the imperial and the colonial. Imperial fraternities were conceptualised in linkage with national categories of 'woman' as nature. The culture/nature, dignified/exotic divide that differentiates imperial women from 'other' women who are still in a state of nature is a significant feature of the construction of hegemonic femininities. On French colonial banknotes, for instance, 'native' women were commonly featured as unclothed 'dusky native maidens' with tropical fruits and lush vegetation, next to their clothed, 'civilised' sisters from the West. Women's bodies (in historically specific ways that were not uniformly played out throughout the empires) operated as boundary markers as territories were marked and nations were forged.

Virgin Territories

The imagery of land as female is a prevalent feature of voyages and discovery. Foreign places were rendered intelligible within a language that imaged the land through the figure of woman's body. The master of all voyagers, Christopher Columbus, for instance, when searching for India in 1492 in the Americas, wrote home to say that the ancient mariners had got the shape of the earth wrong – it wasn't round but instead it was shaped more like a woman's breast with a nipple at the top, towards which he was sailing. In a famous drawing (*c.* 1575) by Jan Ver Straet portraying the discovery of America through the encounter between a man and a woman, Vespucci is shown approaching an indigenous woman who is naked on a hammock. She is in a seductive subservient pose leaning towards him, while he stands erect, fully armoured, with astrolabe, flag and sword, 'gripping the fetish instruments of imperial mastery'. Containing a 'double story of discovery', in the background is shown a cannibal scene of women cooking a human leg, 'redolent not only of male megalomania and imperial aggression but also of male anxiety and paranoia' (McClintock 1995: 25–6). The scene in the foreground depicts advancement on to an available, seductive and uncivilised land, but in the not too far distance lies the possibility of dismemberment: the 'leg roasting on the spit evokes a disordering of the body so castrophic as to be fatal'. What we have before us is an 'anxious vision' representing a crisis in male imperial identity. There is a:

> simultaneous dread of catastrophic boundary *loss* (implosion), associated with fears of impotence and infantalization and attended by *excess* of boundary order and fantasies of unlimited power ... a scene of ambivalence, suspended between an imperial megalomania, with its fantasy of unstoppable rapine – and a contradictory fear of engulfment, with its fantasy of dismemberment and emasculation ... the scene, so neatly gendered, represents a splitting and displacement of a crisis that is, properly speaking, male. (McClintock 1995: 26–7)

Vespucci and Churchill: Boundary Loss

If we return to the scene at the beginning of this chapter, it is possible to link Vespucci's plight with that of Churchill. Could it be that the latter's fantasy of the maleness of his dwelling (the body politic) has nowhere to run (or as he puts 'nothing with which to defend himself') as he fears engulfment, dismemberment and emasculation? The dreaded catastrophic boundary loss (implosion), associated with fears of impotence and infantilisation, forces him to confront his outside when the ordering of his boundaries is arrested by the arrival of a woman MP into the House of Commons (his bathroom), leaving him with a fear of narcissistic disorder. Disrupting the interior space of subjective fantasy, his coherent identity is left fragmented and disorientated – paranoid or dwelling in the productive space of doubt that de-centres his ontological importance?

Churchill's response is one of a type of incident which occurs within institutions, across neighbourhoods or even between national borders when lines are crossed by 'foreign' bodies, 'exemplifying the more or less aggressive defense of a space perceived as violated by an invader' (Burgin 1996: 133). The arrival of hitherto excluded bodies does no doubt allow the habitual functioning of spaces to mutate into a different organisation. At the same time, the movement of a female (foreign) body into his domain sets Churchill running for shelter and lays bear the arbitrary nature of the masculine claim to public space, as a dwelling that is constituted through time requiring continuous repetition, endorsement and protection.

–3–

Dissonant Bodies

The post-colonial presence, where the abstract metaphor of the 'Other' is now metamorphosed into concrete, historical bodies, challenges the screen of universal thought – reason, theory, the West – that has historically masked the presence of a particular voice, sex, sexuality, ethnicity and history, and has only granted the 'Other' a presence in order to confirm its own premises (and prejudices).

Chambers, *Migrancy, Culture, Identity*

I think that there is a profound suggestion in this work that our own turning away from the dark side of our psyche has a lot to do with this relationship that we have physically with the third world or with what we consider to be the less developed world. In a time of global unity it is just not possible to have that kind of division any more and this is the unconscious and the third world brought right into our living room to occupy space and it feels uncomfortable and causes anxiety.

Gormley, *Field for the British Isles*

The multifaceted ways in which the arrival and residence of postcolonials, of first or subsequent generations, have transformed the urban landscapes of the West have, deservedly, attracted the attention of academics across a range of disciplines. The productive energies that have managed to proliferate cultural, social and political developments, in spite of insipid forms of racism, figure in these accounts. New sounds, spoken and musical, foods and smells have all been noted. The challenge posed by this presence to homogeneous notions of place, identity and knowledge has been granted sophisticated attention, most especially in relation to youth cultures and metropolitan city living (Gilroy 1993; Back 1994; Sharma, Hutnyk and Sharma 1996).

The presence of racialised minorities in positions of authority historically and conceptually 'reserved' for specific types of white masculinities has, however, not been granted in-depth attention. This has not been seen to be an ideal locale for noting the postcolonial condition, for elucidating the power of whiteness or for a specific type of doubling of modernity through the presence of a menace that reveals the monstrosity of repressive versions of enlightenment (Du Bois 1989). The complex web of analysis has not travelled from the spontaneous vibrancy found in street life and youth cultures into the rather more restrained air of institutions.[1] As increasing numbers of Black and Asian bodies take up positions within the professions – within politics, academia and the visual arts – there is, in short, a socio-spatial impact to be witnessed. If we are to understand this particular postcolonial condition, the terms of their coexistence require further probing. And our analysis needs to go beyond number-crunching exercises which count (monitor) the quantities of different bodies in the stratified structures of institutions. These endeavours are usually based on banal but dominant versions of multiculturalism which assume that the existence of more bodies of colour in the higher ranks of organisations amounts to and is evidence of diversity and equality. The presence of women or 'black' bodies in the upper layers of institutions should not be taken as a straightforward sign that organisational cultures and structures are drastically changing. In fact, the existence of these hitherto different bodies highlights how certain types of masculinity and whiteness have marked what are often represented as empty, neutral positions that can be filled by any(body). By going beyond simply 'counting heads', we are able to advance a much more complex picture of how whiteness and masculinity are embedded in the character and life of organisations. If we want to grasp how racial and gender discrimination live as latent features of professional occupations, then it is absolutely vital to pay attention to the somatics of these processes.

Reserved Occupational Spaces

Thinking about how we exist in space, Lefebvre has famously noted that it is by means of the body that space is perceived, lived and produced. The proxemics of bodies and space means that 'each living body *is* space and *has* its space: it produces itself in space and it also produces that space' (Lefebvre 2002: 170). Bodies do not simply move through spaces but constitute and are constituted by them. Thus it is possible to see how both the space and the normative bodies of a specific space can become disturbed by the arrival of Black and Asian bodies in occupations which are not historically and conceptually marked out as their 'natural' domain.

The last chapter considered the formation of the public realm and the body politic. Today the exclusionary white male body politic 'has been fragmented and weakened by successive invasions from the excluded' (Gatens 1996: 25). The removal of formal barriers in the last two or three hundred years has meant that legally any(body), male or female, white or 'black', can occupy positions of leadership and authority in the body politic. However, despite the legal right for all bodies to enter these positions, subtle means of inclusion/exclusion continue to informally operate through the designation of the somatic norm. The male body continues to be defined as the ideal type. 'It is still "anthropus" who is taken to be capable of representing the universal type, the universal body. Man is the model and it is his body which is taken for the human body' (Gatens 1996: 24). And, although it is no longer constitutionally and juridically enshrined, nevertheless the white body continues to be the somatic norm (Mills 1997).

Today we have a scenario where the historically embedded relationship between 'reserved' positions and certain social types means that informally the universal 'individual' who is the ideal figure of modernity, found in the state, in bureaucracies and in the professions, still does not include everyone. This coupling is not so set in concrete that it can't be changed, but it is one that weighs heavily upon how those positions are imagined. The positions have a gendered (Gherardi 1995) and racialised symbolism to them. Thus different bodies belonging to 'other' places are in one sense out of place as they are 'space invaders'. Mills speaks of the way in which the 'Racial contract demarcates space, reserving privileged spaces for its first class citizens' (1997: 49). This is certainly the case for privileged spaces in the public realm. It is white men, with a changing classed habitus, who have for hundreds of years filled the higher echelons and over time it is they who have come to be seen as the 'natural' occupants of these positions.

In this chapter the socio-spatial impact of racialised and gendered bodies in occupational spaces for which they are not the normative figures will be gauged through an analytical frame whose reach is much wider than the principal domain of individual institutions. Two fundamental dynamics – disorientation and amplification – are identified as being intrinsic to the ways in which 'new' bodies are encountered. The chapter moves between scenes both in and outside of institutions in order to shed light on the ways in which the processes operate.

Notions of 'the look', 'terror' and the 'monstrous' help us to consider what is disturbed by the arrival or entry of 'new' kinds of bodies in professional occupations which are not historically and conceptually 'reserved' for them. In encounters where the hitherto outside, in a social/ political/psychical sense, is physically on the inside, disorientation and amplification come into play. The institutional sites will be Parliament, Whitehall, academia and the art world. But the spread of the sites that inform the analysis will be much wider. This chapter invites us to consider the resident narratives that disorientation and amplification throw up.

The corporeal dimension of positions of authority is brought to the fore when those whose bodies are not the norm in these places take up these very positions. No doubt there are enormous differences in the cultures of organisations and the qualities required of those who occupy positions in such spaces. However, there are also interesting overlaps in the ways in which authority is granted to bodies across institutions. Professions are forged in particular types of places. Each field has its own peculiarities, histories and institutional identities. The internal life of an organisation is not uniform or homogeneous. Neither is it an isolated phenomenon. Institutions exist in relation to each other. A web of institutional networks which overlap and compete with each other affect the social life of organisations. Their long-distance reach and porous nature create a criss-crossing of global and international networks. Interestingly, though, the universal figure of leadership and representative of humanity continues to be conceptualised in the shadow of the nation. By this, I do not mean that the nation is the most significant player in the determination of political and economic outcomes. Rather, who is seen to have the right to represent is entangled with who is seen to really belong.

An Alien in White Consecrated Space

Standing on the steps outside Westminster, the space from where declarations and speeches are daily made for media reportage, Herman Ousely, the former head of the Commission of Racial Equality, announced on prime-time television news that the atmosphere of Parliament is one where black people feel unwelcome and that he himself, as a black individual, was made to feel as if he were an alien in this space.[2]

Specific scholarly questions had brought me to Westminster and Whitehall. Instead of looking at the dynamics of power by gazing 'down' at working-class and racialised groups, I had chosen to 'research up' (Puwar 1997a). The ethnographic enquiry has from the beginning laid the spotlight, however amicable it may be, on the home-grown working class, colonial populations across the world or the postcolonial in Western cities. Elites[3] themselves have not, however, been the usual objects of anthropological scrutiny seeking to understand 'strangeness'. The power of 'élites' has enabled them to keep ethnographers at a distance. In an interesting twist in epistemic positionalities, now I, the home-grown postcolonial, sought to make what had passed as normal strange by observing the workings of 'race' and gender amongst the ranks of state élites. I wanted to see how certain kinds of whiteness and masculinity were sustained behind the masquerade of disembodied transcendental power, which claimed that all (black, white, male, female, however classed), could, in theory, join.

As I walked through the grand entrance to Parliament I felt a sense of unease with my own bodily arrival in this monument to democracy, nation and Imperial Englishness. A set of stories come with the building. Westminster is one of the 'consecrated relics, traditions and shrines' where 'the very spirit of "History" has laid its blessing on the nation' (Chambers 1990: 16). Since 'histories are made through the selective construction and representation of "tradition" in the public sphere' (Gabriel 1998: 39), mythical tales of distant lands and peoples yielded to imperial power have helped Britain to define itself by processes of dis-identification. Like all foundational myths wrapped up in the making of nations (Taussig 1997), these function as 'a story which locates the origin of the nation, the people and their national character so early that they are lost in the mists of, not "real", but "mythic" time – like basing the definition of the English as "free-born" on the Anglo-Saxon parliament' (Hall, S. 1992: 295).

The building of Westminster, with its Neo-Gothic architecture, high ceilings, arches and acoustics, invites reverence in a similar way to a cathedral, even while it is a heavily surveilled space, especially for non-members. Consensus is rendered 'practical' and 'concrete'. In a monumental space such as a cathedral:

> visitors are bound to become aware of their own footsteps, and listen to the noises, the singing; they must breathe the incense-laden air, and plunge into a particular world, that of sin and redemption; they will partake of an ideology; they will contemplate and decipher the symbols around them; and they will thus, on the basis of their own bodies, experience a total being in a total space. (Lefebvre 2002: 220–1)

Like other monumental spaces Parliament is 'determined by what may not take place there (prescribed/proscribed, scene/obscene)' (Lefebvre 2002: 224). As soon as one steps in, the power of sancticity is practised in the surveilled operations that are a part of the rhythmic rituals of the place. The body starts moving in keeping with the nods and instructions of various gatekeepers, of which there are plenty throughout the building – both as people and as physical structures.

The artwork of Jane and Louise Wilson can help us to begin to think about how such a space is lived in. In a series of installations using video, still photographs and props, the Wilsons consider the mutual constitution of bodies and places within sites of political power. *Parliament* (1999), as a seat of government, is one of their sites (see Figures 3 and 4). Their life-size installations place the viewer in a 'physical encounter' (Wilson and Wilson 1999: 7). Their installation emphasises the disciplinary distinctions that operate in the architectural codes of Parliament. Distinctions between members and strangers are especially noted. The architectural aesthetics, of the minutest detail, as well as more large-scale dimensions, are magnified – the corridors, the doors, the telephone booths, the thick red carpet, as well as the sounds, such as the bell for voting, which coordinates bodies in particular directions at specific times.[4] By dwelling on the mundane domestic details of the least accessible spaces they generate a sense of unease. Their magnified trespassing invites us to consider the absence/presence in the psychic power of architecture.

The Rhythms of Organisations

Interestingly the Wilsons were not allowed to film any people in Parliament. In their own opinion they thought this ruling came out of the fear that as artists they would create some kind of untoward stunt.

While the Wilsons are acutely aware of the proxemics of bodies in space, they don't go as far as thinking about how it is particular types of bodies, with specific habituses, who have made this House their home. The rhythms of organisations affect the type of regimes that prevail in terms of gender and race. In the House, the timing, working procedures, rituals and bodily performances endorse specifically classed notions of masculine Englishness. The bourgeois and gentrified classes 'currently co-exist as inflections ... within hegemonic masculinity' (Connell 1995: 165).

Westminster builds on and contributes to the flows of cathexis established in other places, such as specific public schools, Oxbridge, certain professions, men's clubs, trade unions and pubs and bars. There is an excessive amount of interchange between social and work activities, which helps sustain a system of patronage, gossip and fraternities.

Figure 3 Jane and Louise Wilson, Moses committee room, robing mirror, House of Lords, Parliament, 1999. C-type print mounted on aluminium 180 cm × 180 cm. Courtesy of Lisson Gallery (London)

Hierarchical relations between the upper/middle classes and the working classes of another era are also repeated. Male members themselves no longer wear top hats and tailcoats, but some of the staff are still required to wear the clothing of a previous era. For instance, the porters are men who have to wear breeches and a tailcoat. They are expected to behave in a subservient way. The deference is expressed in the talk and body language of the staff. In the various drinking and eating areas, as one MP put it to me, 'The people that serve you are excessively polite.' Pomp, ceremony and decorated uniforms are also rife here.

Figure 4 Jane and Louise Wilson, Peer's telephone, House of Lords, Parliament, 1999. C-type print mounted on aluminium 180 cm × 180 cm. Courtesy of Lisson Gallery (London)

> I always think that the House of Commons itself, in its corridors when you sort of look at the lobbies and things, it's a cross really between a cathedral and a public boys' school and that's still the ethos that pervades the place ... it's the whole history of Parliament. It was a place where gentlemen with a gentlemen's profession came after they had had a good lunch and really in lots of ways that kind of ethos has not changed. We still have people dressed up in eighteenth-century costumes and stockings and buckle shoes. I mean its a bizarre institution, it's one in which people, men, well almost entirely men, are completely addicted to this kind of ancient regime and it pervades everything. (Labour Party female MP)

It is into this atmosphere that women MPs and Black and Asian MPs arrive. And it is no wonder that Ousely declared that he felt like an alien.

Back in 1919 the first female MP, Nancy Astor, found the House so uncomfortable that it is reported that she never went into any part of the House except the Chamber and her own room (Vallance 1979). Grosz states that 'The more one disinvests one's own body from ... [a] ... space, the less able one is to effectively inhabit that space as one's own' (Grosz 2001: 9). Nancy Astor certainly disinvested herself. Today women MPs occupy the various spaces of Parliament in a much fuller way. They enter the bars and the tearooms, even if it is still sometimes with an air of trepidation. After all, the masculinity of Parliament is still reproduced through the sheer numbers of men, specific social/work activities – such as smoking cigars, drinking, the topic of conversations – all of which contributes to a masculine culture. Like other masculine cultures at work, this atmosphere 'can make women feel, without being told in so many words, "you are out of place here"' (Cockburn 1991: 65). At the same time, though, the arrival of women MPs is opening up the space, however slowly, for 'a different inhabitation' (Grosz 2001: 9). The presence of white women MPs has increased (Williams 1989; Eagle *et al.* 1998; Childs 2001; Mackay 2001), even though it is far from being the norm (see www.parliament.gov.uk for the latest statistics and portfolios).

The Look

The entry of a black female, or male, figure is, however, received quite differently. This presence is still capable of inducing a state of ontological anxiety. It disturbs a particular 'look'.

Commenting on the epistemic position from which the Western, masculine, rational universal leader has historically developed an assured sense of himself, Irigaray observes that this has been a place from where, 'in his room or in his study, sometimes enjoying a fire fancied to be burning in baroque curls of smoke or else gazing out through the/his window' (1985a: 212–13), supported by woman, he has conducted the 'serene contemplation of Empire' (1985a: 136). These leaders have enjoyed their 'fancied fires' in the solitude of their study, or the company of like men, away from women and less civilised colonials or ex-colonials. Psychic and physical boundaries have been implicit to the sense of Europeanness, and more specifically the sense of who men of knowledge and leadership are as well as where they are placed. Well, now, albeit one by one and ever so slowly, those postcolonials have walked right into those rooms from which these men of 'wisdom' have looked out on to the world. The previously colonised enter because they have the legal right to enter. The formal right and increased movement do not, however, mean that they don't remain unexpected and even uninvited guests.

Empire was contemplated in such a way that its gaze put into play a corporeal racial schema of alien other(s) which helped to glue collectivities of whiteness with a superior sense of their 'natural' right to occupy privileged spaces of institutional representation on both a national and an international scale. Commenting on the arrival of a black female body in one of the most intimate spaces of Westminster – the Smoking Room – Tony Banks (Labour MP) offers some telling observations. He notes:

> It is rather like one of those leather-enrobed London clubs in Pall Mall. I took Diane Abbott in there soon after she was elected and the response from the habitués was electrifying. They didn't need to say a word, both Diane and I knew the question. [In other words, what is she doing in here?] But she wasn't a cleaner. (*Sunday Telegraph*, 28 January 1996)

It is worth dwelling on the 'look' that darted across this white, cigar-filled, masculine space to receive this black female body. Here we have an encounter that bears remarkable resemblance to the now widely cited look once experienced by Frantz Fanon. Being 'supersaturated with meaning', there is 'a received stock of already-interpreted images of black bodies' (Gooding-Williams 1993: 158, 165) that kicks into place in a particular reading of the black/female body.[5] Allotted a place out there somewhere, in the hidden labour of public domestic work, outside of the 'seat of power', the arrival of a black female body triggers a racialised 'shameful livery put together by centuries of incomprehension' (Fanon 1986: 14). She is automatically classified, primitivised, domesticated and decivilised, categories that are all too familiar in processes of racialisation, be they theoretical acts or everyday interactions (Fanon 1986: 32).

Within the area of 'race' and racism Fanon's work has been a source of analytical inspiration to innumerable scholars (Gordon 1995; Read 1996; Macey 2000, 2002), especially the notion of the look.[6] It is, however, surprising how little use has been made of his work for helping us to understand the dynamics of institutional racism. Arriving in France as a psychiatrist in the 1950s from the French colony Martinique, Fanon, as a 'black' colonial figure, or, as he puts it in the language of the time, a 'negro', is confronted by the exclamation 'Look, a Negro!' (Fanon 1986: 109). The most vivid and subsequently most cited image is provided in an encounter he had with a little girl on the street. Of this he writes:

'Look, a Negro!' It was an external stimulus that flicked over me as I passed by. I made a tight smile. 'Look, a Negro!' It was true. It amused me. 'Look, a Negro!' The circle was drawing a bit tighter. I made no secret of my amusement. 'Mama, see the Negro! I'm frightened!' Frightened! Frightened! Now they were beginning to be afraid of me. I made up my mind to laugh myself to tears, but laughter had become impossible. I could no longer laugh, because I already knew that there were legends, stories, history and above all historicity ... Then, assailed at various points, the corporeal schema crumbled, its place taken by a racial epidermal schema. (1986: 112)

The somatic dimensions of racialisation are central to the incisive analysis Fanon offers of what this *look* does to the 'black' subject/ body.[7] It is a look he observes as taking place, often without verbal communication, in everyday spaces in the city (bars, cafés and trains), as well as more enclosed institutional spaces (lecture halls, doctor's surgeries and psychiatric hospitals).

Reflecting on 'the look' in detail, Fanon notes: 'the movements, the attitudes, the glances of the other fixed me there, in the sense in which a chemical solution is fixed by a dye'. He says, 'Sealed into that crushing objecthood', the look 'imprisoned me'. The force of the racist episteme is imprinted on the body. Fanon asks: 'What else could it be for me but an amputation, an excision, a haemorrhage that spattered my whole body with black blood?' A 'historico-racial schema' below the corporeal schema had, he says 'woven me out of a thousand details, anecdotes, stories'. From the 'racial epidermal schema' he had been assigned ethnic characteristics, through which, he says: 'I was battered down by tom-toms, cannibalism, intellectual deficiency, fetishism, racial defects, slave-ships, and above all else, above all: "Sho' good eatin"' (Fanon 1986: 109–12). He was 'classified', 'tucked away'.

The look operated as a 'weight', which, he says, 'burdened me' and 'challenged my claims' on the world: on where he could be and what he could be. Locating himself 'as a body in the middle of a spatial-temporal world' which placed him through a racialised schema, he notes, 'I was told to stay within bounds, to go back where I belonged.' He cries out: 'dissected under white eyes, the only real eyes. I am *fixed*' (Fanon 1986: 110–16).

Disorientation

The claims 'black' bodies make on institutions by occupying spaces they are not expected to be in are constantly challenged by a look which abnormalises their presence and locates them, through the workings of racialised framings, as belonging elsewhere. It is important to note, though, that, at the same time as the black body is fixed by a white gaze, the white gaze itself is disorientated by the close proximity of these foreign bodies. Their very presence, as 'equal' members rather than as service staff (porters, cleaners, clerks and nannies), who take up a different rhythm in the occupation of space, challenges the ways in which racialised bodies have been categorised and fixed. Significantly, both the way in which the 'other' has been fixed and the construction of self in relation to this image are troubled; there is a disturbance of a certain order. A racialised episteme is interrupted. Thinking back to the scene in the Smoking Room in Parliament, the occupation of what has been dressed up as a 'universal' position of authority, even though we know it is crafted for particular bodies, or, rather, precisely because it is a black body, represents a dissonance; a jarring of framings that confuses and disorientates. It is a menacing presence that disturbs and interrupts a certain white, usually male, sense of public institutional place.

Disorientation is one of the processes that bring to the fore the space-invader status of racialised bodies in privileged occupational positions. It is revealing of how specific bodies have been constructed out of the imagination of authority. Soon after being elected, Bernie Grant reflected on how his 'black' body was constantly questioned as a presence in the House of Commons, revealing a mismatch between the category MP and the category black. He remarked:

> One of the catering staff was shocked to see me in the catering establishment and demanded to know what I was doing there until they found out that I was a Member of Parliament.
>
> I was going into a lift and this guy said to me 'oh well, only Members can go in the lift' and I said I was a Member and then he recognised me. (Cited in Howe 1988: 9)

Once a black MP is known and becomes a familiar face, then their physical presence won't be openly quizzed. However, when a new unknown member joins, their presence will be interrogated in the same way, because they don't have an undisputed right to occupy the space. They are seen to be suspiciously out of place. To use Fanon's vocabulary, they are burdened by the claims black bodies can make on the world. In contrast, a white body is much more likely to be automatically accepted; their right to enter and exist is not an issue in quite the same way.[8]

Disorientation Across Space and Bodies

Westminster is a particularly peculiar institution and the encounters that take place here are quite specific to the archaic, crusty nature of this space. No doubt the architecture, the atmosphere and the talk that resounds across the Chamber, between the pillars of the corridors, the clinking of double whiskies, the tapping of heels on the heavy stone floors and the scent of cigars do make the encounter with 'black' bodies very distinctive. However, the disorientation caused by black bodies in positions of authority in the public realm is not unique to this institution. It is found across many other institutions. It even resides in what is characterised as the absolute pinnacle of rationality, the senior civil service, where in theory there is no room for the consideration of bodies because everything is mind. Here, too, black bodies in senior roles are noticed as matter out of place. This is not surprising, given that the more a position or occupation is imbued with the lofty air of universality, the less viable it is for these places to be the natural habitat of Black or Asian bodies.

The few senior 'black' civil servants who do exist in the higher ranks have found that their colleagues are often surprised to find a non-white person in a senior position. Reflecting on this experience, the civil servants mentioned that their presence in the more senior ranks 'throws people' and that their colleagues do a 'double take'. Commenting on what it is like to attend a work-related social function, one 'black' civil servant observed: 'you feel that they are noticing you and can't quite work out what you are doing there. It's like going into a pub in Cornwall. Every one turns around when you open the door ... that sort of feeling.' In a sense it is this 'What are you doing here?' look that abnormalises the presence of these 'black' bodies. It illustrates how positions of authority are embodied. At the same time, the coming together of bodies and spaces which have been juxtaposed induces a whole set of anxieties. In one sense, it represents a psychical somatic collision. The presence of these bodies in this place defies expectations. People are 'thrown' because a whole world-view is jolted. What they see before their eyes – postcolonial bodies in highly accomplished positions, right in the heart of whiteness – seizes their categorisations of space/body. They will no doubt try to clobber these rather unusual creatures into long-established images in the archive of imperial memory.

Disorientation does also occur along the lines of gender. But it is not as acute as it is with 'race'. Scenarios of the following kind, reported by a woman who entered the fast stream of the civil service in the 1960s, are far less likely to occur today:[9]

> There were certain things that I felt odd about. I remember, on my second day, there was a knock on the door, and there were two people who'd joined the year ahead of me, as fast-streamers, and they'd basically come to have a look, you know, and they hadn't seen a woman trainee around, and they came to peer and went away again, rather frightened and then inviting me out to lunch sort of thing!

A significant levelling in the number of women entering the senior civil service has occurred over time. Nevertheless, the presence of women at the apex of the hierarchy can still occasion disorientation because women are still not the normative figure of authority at the higher levels of the bureaucracy. Notwithstanding departmental variations in numbers, cultures and structures, a head of department relayed an account to me which clearly illustrates how man is the unspecified somatic norm and the presence of a woman can be a disappointment:

> people are very surprised when they find me here. One lady came once to visit me, and she'd been reading the Department's Annual Report, and, of course, it kept referring to 'she', 'she' you know from time to time, not all the time. And when she came in, she looked at me, and she said 'Good Lord!' she said, 'You're a woman!' So I said, 'Well, what did you expect?' She said 'Well', she said, 'You won't believe this', she said. 'But I was convinced that the [Head of the Department] had to be a man, that when I read "she, she, she" in the text, I assumed that it was some peculiarity of this particular post, that the [Head of the Department] was always called "she", although he was a "he".'

In the next chapter I shall discuss how the 'double take' leads on to yet further 'takes' when gendered bodies speak, leading to the menace of their presence becoming even more exacerbated. For now I would like to stay with how the very taking up of a social space from where the universal subject speaks by a racialised subject is a cause of anxiety in institutions. It is worth pondering on why they engender a 'double take'. Why are they, in some small way, a shock to the system?

Disorientation in Academia

If we turn to the world of academia, it is possible to see how the placing of racialised 'other' bodies in the position of subject rather than that of

the usual objects of knowledge calls into question the territorial demarcations that mark the identity of the academic, especially the all-seeing
globe-trotting academic. Regardless of how amicable academics are to
other cultures and people, the sharing of the seat of power (knowledge)
with those one studies can be an experience that very easily 'throws'
institutional positionalities and runs the risk of causing ontological
anxiety.

Claude Lévi-Strauss provides a remarkable case in point. While Lévi-
Strauss was doing his fieldwork on American ethnology in New York,
an assured sense of ontological importance was in a particular encounter
destabilised. Sitting in the reading-room of New York Public Library,
where he was doing research for his *Elementary Structures of Kinship*, he
was thrown by the sight of a feathered Indian with a Parker pen, because
the 'Indian' is located by Lévi-Strauss, despite his anti-racism, along
with a whole bank of knowledge, in another time frame, a past that is
outside a particular narrative of modernity. James Clifford observes that:
'In modern New York an Indian can appear only as a survival or a kind
of incongruous parody' (cited in Chow 1993: 28). Thus what he sees
before his eyes is 'odd' for Lévi-Strauss because, for him, the specialist,
the image before him does not fit the 'authentic' image of an Indian. As
Chow says, 'What confronts the Western scholar is the discomforting
fact that the natives are no longer staying in their frames' (1993: 28).

The arrival of a feathered Indian with a Parker pen (an instrument
of technology that has written the world into being) into the reading-
room (a place from where the world is contemplated) is discomforting
not merely because the analytical categories of this scholar are not
sophisticated enough to fit the image, but, more importantly, because
the very identity of the intellectual as sovereign knower of the world is
called into question. By moving out of the frames through which s/he is
known, the 'native' is not just dislodging how s/he has been classified,
but also how the Western scholar has framed himself. The self-image or
ontological being of the masters of the universe, epistemically speaking,
causes a double take. This is what is really shocking. This is a case
where the identity of the scholar who goes 'tramping around the world'
as a universal figure of academic knowledge is (Probyn 1993), to put it
mildly, put out of sync.

What becomes evident in this encounter is that there is a psychic/
social/physical territorial boundary which marks the separation between
the ever so interesting and even 'wise' cultures of 'other' worlds and the
place of the Western intellectual who brings the voice of reason to each
of his collections. The boundary that gives a place and position to the

Western intellect as the torch bearer of enlightenment is now threatened by the sight in front of Lévi-Strauss. Others too can clasp the instruments and become purveyors of knowledge.[10]

The crisis/puzzled thoughts that are induced in Lévi-Strauss are perhaps not surprising given the long historical epistemological/ontological bond which has constituted the sovereignty of the European subject (discussed in the last chapter via the plight of Churchill). While identifying themselves with reason, modernity and the ability to enact the universal and not just the particular, at the same time others were/are dis-identified from these capacities. The entry of 'the native' in the studies, offices and boardrooms troubles notions of self and other as they relate to who is the sovereign subject as well as the sovereign 'eye'. The latent categories and boundaries that tacitly inform who has the right to look, judge and represent start, ever so slightly, to falter.[11]

Uncomfortable Encounters

The ever-increasing proximity of people on the other side of the world to the geopolitical centre is able to generate an uncomfortable confrontation that forces an evacuation of epistemological/ontological assurance. The complexity of this process is captured most vividly through a sculptural work by the artist Paul Gormley titled *The Field*. The potential of the sheer physical presence, arrival and entry of particular bodies in a social space they are not expected to be in to engender unease is brought home to us through a very simple installation. This work unsettles taken-for-granted positionalities and provokes viewers to open up for questioning their own place in the world.

Gormley has created a series of fields (see Figure 5a and b).[12] These consist of hand-sized figures, with two holes for their eyes, made from baked clay. Thousands of these figures densely pack the floor of a whole room, which consists of nothing else but white walls and lighting. Importantly, all the figures vary very slightly in height but each is less than a foot high and faces the entrance to the room, the point from which the audience views them. The viewer is blocked from inspecting the whole gallery space by the presence of the figures, whose gaze, through the two holes in the head, looks up quizzically. The figures appeal to onlookers to reflect upon the boundaries which locate and construct a privileged position in the world. The point from which the viewer looks and asserts authority is a question that is raised by the presence of these figures.

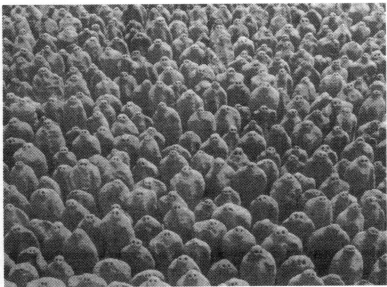

Figures 5(a) and (b) Antony Gormley, *The Field* (1991). Courtesy of Jay Jopling/White Cube (London).

As audiences tower over the figures from a platform of authority, the intense upward ironic gaze of these figures tugs at the coherence of this superior positioning.[13] Discussing how *The Field* is a mesmerising entity that attempts to move a taken-for-granted position of privilege, Gormley states:

> There is a trick that the work plays – life becomes its subject – we previously would have entered a gallery to share the space of the gallery with works and, in some way, aesthetically be possessed or possess those works. With Field, the space is entirely occupied by the work and the work then seems to make us its subject; seems to make life its subject so we are, in a way, invaded and it's not only that this space, the art gallery space, that we thought was ours has been invaded but we are also invaded: we are made the object of the art's scrutiny. These gazes look to us to find their place; they have a place but it's a place that we can't enter and they are looking to the space of consciousness inside us as their rightful promised land and that's a strange feeling ... This invasion of physical space, which you could also think of as a kind of infection, it is a physical metaphor for personal space. (1996: 61–2)

We can use the way in which Gormley has brought together space, body, territoriality and the gaze to look at race and gender in institutions. When racialised figures walk into historically white spaces as figures of authority, they generate unease. The boundaries that have contributed to a privileged sense of whiteness are jarred. This confrontation of the previously outside now on the inside contains the potential to move people out of entrenched positions.[14] But it can also be received as a terrorising threat.

Amplification of Numbers

Gormley stressed the sense in which the audience who look at the figures in *The Field* feel that their physical/personal space has been invaded. In institutional settings the numbers of 'black' bodies entering the higher echelons, or the routes to the higher echelons, are by no means in their thousands. Unlike Gormley's figures they do not fill the space *en masse*. However, while 'black' bodies are still statistically small in numbers, they are perceived as bodies that disturb the normal institutional landscape. Moreover, their numbers become amplified and they come to threateningly fill the space in much larger numbers than they literally do. This means that a sprinkling of two or three Black and Asian bodies rapidly become exaggerated to four or seven. And, interestingly, even a single body can be seen to be taking up more physical space than it actually occupies.

The reception of women in classically male spaces can bring on similar dynamics to the arrival of the 'third world' that fills galleries in Gormley's *Field*. The MP Sally Keeble says the treatment of the class of 1997 women who entered the House reminded her 'of the way people treat asylum-seekers, seeing themselves as "flooded". It felt like an institution that was bracing himself for something alien' (cited in Campbell 2003). Thus an amplification of numbers is also evidenced along the lines of gender as well as race, although it is much more of an acute phenomenon with race. When, for instance, appointments are made, women in senior positions are more likely to be noticed and counted, in a way that men are not. A woman senior civil servant recalled one such scenario:

they're counting, they're not doing it consciously, but you can sort of, you can sense it's a consideration ... and this comes up quite often: 'Well we've already got two women' or something. 'And it'll look a bit odd if we appoint a third woman.' You say, 'You mean like it was odd when you appointed the third man so and so?' And they laugh in a rather embarrassed way. 'Well, yes, of course, of course.' But that was a subconscious thought, there are two women, so we don't want to look as if we're biased. And they just don't see that the last five were men, and nobody thought that was bad.

Intrinsic to the dynamics involved in the amplification of numbers is the phenomenon of visibility, threat and terror. As bodies out of place or unexpected bodies, they are highly conspicuous. This is a visibility that comes from not being the norm. It is a process that is not all that different from the way in which racialised minorities are visible on the street, and especially in particular locations heavily demarcated as white places. Lest we think that what is involved here is simply a curiosity about newcomers, strangers or the unknown, coupled with the issue of numbers is the question of terror. The amplification occurs not only because they are unknown, but precisely because they are already 'known' in ways which are seen to threaten the spurious claims on space for a coherent superior identity. There is a terror of numbers, a fear of being swamped.[15] The dread of being displaced from an identity that has placed the white subject as being central to the world propels one to be constantly vigilant as to the activities of the figures that make it uncomfortable to hold on to this position. The vigilance borders on the paranoiac, an anxiety that unleashes its own so-called 'protective' symbolic and physical violence.

Amplification of Presence: Wired Up as Terror

The transposition of the existence of specific types of bodies into a threatening terror has a long lineage of racialised imaginings which have been in operation across continents and countries. Once again, it is useful to briefly turn to the insights drawn from the everyday wanderings of Frantz Fanon as a black man in the streets of France (which gives his flânerie a significantly different hue from that of Baudelaire). Fanon speaks of how on a 'white winter day' his cold shaking body becomes a body of terror through a 'look', whose retinal function is connected to a discursive network of stories of barbarism, horror and disgust:

> look, a nigger, it's cold, the nigger is shivering, the nigger is shivering because he is cold, the little boy is trembling because he is afraid of the nigger, the nigger is shivering with cold, that cold that goes through your bones, the handsome little boy is trembling because he thinks that the nigger is quivering with rage, the little white boy throws himself into his mother's arms. Mama, the nigger's going to eat me up. (Fanon 1986: 113–14)

The automatic mutation of a black body in movement – shaking, laughing, calling or touching – into something to be feared occurs through the infinitesimal everyday interactions and exchanges as bodies pass by each other and glances shoot across streets, trains and executive meetings. 'Black' bodies are known as belonging to other places, outside civil places. Once they enter these realms of the 'civilised', they represent the unknown and the potentially monstrous.

During the age of enlightenment and the age of reason (Warner 2000), human variations of the monster 'became a favourite metaphor to express new anxieties surrounding the self, and its conjoined twin, the other' (Kearney 2003: 118). This is particularly evident in impressions of other 'savage lands' living in a 'state of nature' (which were then, of course, colonised). For instance, Vespucci's discovery of the unknown territory of America by Jan Ver Straet (*c.* 1575), discussed in Chapter 2, represents an anxious vision of boundary loss and a fear of engulfment in the encounter with cannibals (McClintock 1995: 26–7). One thing that monsters do is defy conventional boundaries. Today 'black' bodies in senior positions also defy conventions. They have entered spaces where their bodies are neither historically or conceptually the 'norm'. For those for whom the whiteness of these spaces provides a comforting familiarity, the arrival of racialised members can represent the monstrous. Why? Because 'monsters scare the hell out of us and remind us that we don't know who we are. They bring us to no man's land and fill us with fear and trembling' (Kearney 2003: 117). As the incongruous, they invade the normative location of bodies in space. They bring with them indefinite possibilities. They threaten the status quo. Whether they threaten it or not, that is what is feared. Their movements, postures and gestures are closely watched for any untoward behaviour. Racialised optics remain suspicious of these bodies out of place. They could represent an organisational terror, however muted it may be.

The invisible move from a gesturing black body, to threat and then to 'protective terror', was played out in slow motion by the legal ruling on the beating of Rodney King by police in the United States. In court a video offered an eyewitness account of the police violently beating Rodney King. When charged with this, the defence attorneys for the police argued that they were only defending themselves from King, who was the real danger as he had an intention to injure the police officers. The jury in Simi Valley found this reading viable. Deconstructing how it was possible for the jury to interpret the visual evidence of the police enacting severe violence on King as proof of King being a moment away from exerting violence on the police, Judith Butler states that it was feasible to construe King as an agent of violence rather than a victim of it because the attorneys were able to wire in to a familiar white paranoia of blackness, which made them 'see' things in the video that were not there. Most notable is the scene where 'King's palm turned away from his body, held above his own head, is read *not* as self-protection but as the incipient moments of a physical threat'. She asks, 'How do we account for this *reversal* of gesture and intention in terms of a racial schematization of the visible field?' (1993b: 16).

> The video was used as 'evidence' to support the claim that the frozen black male body on the ground receiving the blows was himself producing those blows, about to produce them, was himself the imminent threat of a blow and, therefore, was himself responsible for the blows he received. That body thus received those blows which were that body in its essential gestures, even as the one gesture that body can be seen to make is to raise its palm outward to stave off the blows against it. According to this racist episteme, he is hit in exchange for the blows he never delivered, but which he is, by virtue of his blackness, always about to deliver. (Butler 1993b: 18–19)

Within a racialised circuit of paranoia, King's body emblematises the fear of the black male body and white vulnerability. The predominantly white jury assume 'the projection of their own aggression, and the subsequent regarding of that projection as an external threat'. We thus have in evidence a 'white paranoia which projects the intention to injure that it itself enacts' (Butler 1993b: 19–22).

Amplification of presence is intrinsic to the way in which terror/numbers/paranoia work together in this scenario. Even though King is just one body against several armed police officers, he is presented by the defence attorneys as being larger than life. His presence is expanded in size and proportion and hence the relentless blows he receives. The monstrous proportions he is apportioned accentuate the threat he poses, as well as justifying the vicious treatment that is meted out.

Amplification: Organisational Terror

How the existence of 'black' bodies in relatively élite positions within institutions can be perceived as a threat is clearly of quite a different order from how the body of Rodney King was perceived to justify further state violence. An appreciation of the differentiated degrees of terror is no doubt called for. Those black bodies who manage to get into positions of authority in institutions are in one sense deemed 'safe'. They have gone through the vetting and selection procedures that monitor entry to the professions. They have passed the surveillance tests (discussed in Chapters 6 and 7). Furthermore, by existing in particular institutions, they themselves have some degree of investment, however ambivalent it may be, in the professions they have chosen. They can be perceived as being 'terrifying', but they clearly don't represent the direct physical violent terror assigned to Rodney King's body. The terror they represent is expressed differently. It is much more benign. Their presence is ordinary even as it is peculiar, but it is also ever bordering on being suspiciously alarming. They risk being viewed as an 'organisational terror'.

Thinking about security, cultural and spatial, in an institutional context, there is a fear that 'black' bodies will alter the look of the institution, and they won't fully respect the norms or values as they will be eager for change, especially in terms of 'race'. Most importantly, there is a fear that they will displace the security from which the white figure of authority (usually he, but sometimes she) has spoken.

The process of amplification is further exacerbated if the 'black' bodies converse with each other in close proximity. In fact, they only have to be sitting together at a meeting or standing together in a lobby area before a series of leaps of imagination see a potential renegade movement in the making. Suspicions of whistle-blowing and untoward thought can transform a straightforward conversation about the trip into work into collusion. Laughter and revelry may very easily become a disturbance. A cohort becomes a swarm that invites vigilance. What is feared is an organisational alliance. And, indeed, if 'black' staff do decide to form a self-autonomous group on issues of racism, then they will invite even further suspicion. In most professions there is a taboo attached to naming racism, let alone organising against it. Those who openly take it up as an internal issue, in one way or another, mark themselves out as potentially risky bodies.

The easy assumption that the coming together of these bodies is a potential act of aggression which intends to exclude others from its fraternal cathexis is a projection of an insecurity of losing the central and superior place of whiteness in the structuring of organisations and positions of authority. Thus its own hegemonic cathexis gets projected on to the social groupings of 'others', who are read as having already created exclusive collectivities even before they actually have. This is then used to justify the taboo that surrounds the naming of 'race' and racism in professional occupations. Fearing the loss of the glue that binds whiteness, any sign of a black collectivity is likely to be read as a tight-knit 'community' in the making that threatens the general collectivity of the profession. Naming race is seen to give race prominence in an organisation where it is considered to make no difference. The normativity of whiteness thus remains invisible. A 'black' gathering or support group can be assigned a potentially monstrous aura. These racialised bodies are assigned a territoriality, so that the territorial markings that come with whiteness are, like the blows to Rodney King's body, deflected and projected on to the other.

Similar dynamics come into play along the lines of gender. The presence of two or more women in male spaces can also be viewed as a potential organisational territorial block. Metaphors of war, battle, territories and invasions can be found amongst the male talk (humour) of the female presence amongst their ranks. The threat that these women may actually form some kind of organisational alliance (regiment) is what is feared, because it will displace the existing masculine organisational forms that manage to stay unmarked and invisible. A woman in the senior civil service remarked:

> I remember the day, just after I got the promotion. I mean there was me, and there was one other Grade 3 ... And I met one of my male colleagues ... he was actually a very nice man, comes up to me and he said that the 'monstrous regiment of women marches on'. And I said 'What?' [Laughs] 'There are two of us?'

In the 1997 general election when the numbers of women MPs doubled to 120, leaving men a mere 500, a Labour back-bencher declared to the press: 'I don't know what they do to the Tories but, by God, they frighten me … Just don't know what to make of them.' A Conservative MP expressed that he feared that the women 'will start meddling in defence policy, increasing the aid budget and deploying peace-keeping troops everywhere' (cited in the *Spectator*, 24 May 1997).

The dissonance caused by the arrival of women and racialised minorities in privileged occupational spaces unleashes shock and surprise. Their entry causes disorientation and terror. The threat they are seen to pose amplifies their presence. As 'space invaders' they represent a potential organisational terror. They are thus highly visible bodies that by their mere presence invite suspicion and surveillance.

–4–

(In)Visible Universal Bodies

> ... *racially* invisible – the ghosts of modernity, whites could assume power
> as the norm of humanity, as the naturally given. Unseen racially, that is
> seen as racially marked – or seen precisely as racially unmarked – whites
> could be everywhere.
>
> Goldberg, *Racial Subjects*

The idea that professional positions have job descriptions drawn up in
neutered, neutral and colourless terms holds an enormous power. The
story is that, having arrived at the door to the summit of whichever
chosen profession, that is, those who are lucky enough to arrive at this
point, people will then flourish, develop and be respected, regardless of
gender, 'race' or class background. Received and treated as any other
fellow human being (colleague); their professional identity as an artist,
writer, lawyer, politician, United Nations inspector, senior civil servant
or academic will be the main point of engagement.

Of course, it is correct to say that there are no explicit barriers barring
women, Black or Asian people from taking up positions in the professions;
and the fact that they do enter, in however small numbers, evidences this.
The promise of a realm of pure reason, rationality and mind is at the same
time, although it is unacknowledged, deeply and specifically corporeal
in terms of which bodies can bear the torch of reason and leadership: a
reminder (or remainder) of the exclusive and differentiated hierarchies
which have formed the public realm (as discussed in Chapter 2), and of
how an ideal figure of modernity continues to be an undeclared corporeal
norm, against whom others are measured.

The Universal Human Form

The subtle and nuanced ways in which racial inequality continues
alongside official claims to equality between all in liberalism are
captured by Kobena Mercer (1995) in his commentary on a sculpture by

Charles Cordier titled *Fraternité*. This sculpture, which is taken to be a representation of formal equality between black and white, displays two cherubs – one black and one white – who reach towards each other for an embrace. Mercer notes that, despite the fact that this artifice has been made to honour the principle of equality, inequality is actually implicit in the display of fraternity in the sculpture. He argues:

> While it enacts the sentimental trope repeated today in the exhortation that 'ebony and ivory get together in perfect harmony' upon closer examination of the subtle disposition of these two black and white figures it is the black cherub who actively moves towards the slightly superior, upright, posture of the white one, thus positioned as the universal human from which the other is differentiated. (1995: 25)

The ability to pass as the 'universal human' is an incredibly powerful location precisely because positions within the public realm are normed as being universal and disembodied. And yet we know that only certain bodies are assigned as having the capacity to be universal. Commenting on how representation, leadership and whiteness coalesce, Richard Dyer states: 'The idea of leadership suggests both a narrative of human progress and the peculiar quality to effect it. Thus white people lead humanity forward because of their temperamental qualities of leadership: will power, far sightedness, energy' (1997: 14).

There is a co-constitutive relationship between the body of the universal human and universal space(s). Professional spaces are exalted as being organised by the rules of universal reason. In precious professional circles, the character Mr Spock, from *Star Trek*, represents the archetypal figure; he discards all that is not logical. In fact, he is so logical that he himself states: 'I am incapable of emotion.' A defining feature of the universal human is that he brings us a transcendental vision. He embodies the age of reason, culture and science over and above emotion, nature and myth. Scientific rationality itself is seen to be a defining feature of modern bureaucracies, an integral component of professionalism. Bureaucrats in particular, that is, senior civil servants in Westminster, Brussels or the United Nations, are represented as being at the absolute pinnacle of organisational rationality. There is, in fact, a distinction between specialists, such as lawyers, economists or doctors, for instance, and the more superior generalist figures found in the bureaucracies, who guard the public domain with a god-like balanced, panoramic view of matters across the land. All of them, though – as professionals – are, like the classic Mr Spock scientist, represented as the producers of unbiased, value-free information and advice. Working in adherence to scientific procedure, these bureaucratic bodies, like their close cousins who work in laboratories, are exalted as the guardians of impartiality, in a world riddled by particularisms.[1]

Disembodied Institutional Narratives

An overwhelming feature of this majestic story is that the universal figure is disembodied; the body is irrelevant to this positionality. Being pure mind, their bodies are of no consequence. So whether they are men or women or from a specific class or race is considered irrelevant; they are blank individuals who act out their duties and responsibilities. The capacity to be unmarked by one's body, in terms of race, gender or for that matter any other social feature, is a key component of what makes a universal body. It is a 'privileged position' that is 'reserved' for those who are not bedraggled by the humble shackles of nature, emotion and, in effect, the bodily, allowing them to escape into the higher realms of rationality and mind. The conceptualisation of liberal bureaucracy as a place of ideas, abstracted from the body, is extremely pervasive within public discourse. Not surprisingly, this institutional narrative is also a defining feature of the identity and work ethic of professionals themselves.

In an enormously influential spin on the tale of the public realm, the body has been repressed. As noted in Chapter 2, the repression of embodiment is absolutely key to the characterisation of the abstract 'individual', since the 'universalism of the category of the "individual" can be maintained only as long as the abstraction from the body is maintained' (Pateman 1995: 50). Interestingly, though, in the folds of the spin we find that 'the body is only irrelevant when it's the (white) male body' (Mills 1997: 53). The vital ingredient, a transcendence of the body, is a capacity that women and non-whites are not associated with. Their physicality remains visible.

The Power of Invisibility

When a body is emptied of its gender or race, this is a mark of how its position is the privileged norm. Its power emanates from its ability to be seen as just normal, to be without corporeality. Its own gender or race remains invisible; a non-issue. With 'whiteness' 'defined as an absence of colour' (Williams 1997a), whiteness exists as an unmarked normative position. Similarly the male body is invisible as a sexed entity. Its absence of gender entitles it to take up the unmarked normative locale. The fact that whiteness is also a colour and a racialised position remains a non-issue precisely because race is ex-nominated. Left unnamed and unseen, invisibility in this context is clearly a place of power. Invisibility is, as noted by Burgin, a general instrument of power:

> Roland Barthes once defined the bourgeoisie as 'the social class which does not want to be named.' ... By refusing to be named, the bourgeois class represents itself and its interests as a universal norm, from which anything else is a deviation ... *White* however has the strange property of directing our attention to color while in the very same movement it exnominates itself *as* a color. For evidence of this we need to look no further than to the expression 'people of color,' for we know very well that this means 'not White.' ... To speak of the color of skin is to speak of a body. 'People of color' are embodied people. To have no color is to have no body. The body denied here however is a very particular body. (1996: 130–1)

The ideal representatives of humanity are those who are not marked by their body and who are, in an embodied sense, invisible. This is a privilege which is not, as we have seen in the discussion so far in this chapter, available to those who are considered to be of colour, who are considered to be marked and highly visible. The last chapter considered the socio-spatial impact of highly conspicuous racialised and gendered bodies in places where they are not the norm. This chapter will pay attention to how processes of invisibility and visibility help us to understand the nuanced dynamics of subtle forms of exclusion as well as the basis of differentiated inclusion. They are both insiders and outsiders, who are of the world they work in and at the same time not totally of it. They have a social position in occupational space that is tenuous, a contradictory location marked by dynamics of in/visibility.

Issues of in/visibility are manifested in a series of social dynamics. This chapter identifies them as being: a burden of doubt, infantilisation, super-surveillance and a burden of representation. Simultaneously they are seen without being seen; complicated processes of strait-jacketing grant recognition within very select parameters. On the one hand, they are highly visible as conspicuous bodies, for whom specific slots are made as representatives of particular rather than general forms of humanity. On the other hand, they are invisible as they struggle to be seen as competent and capable. Questions of the marked and invisible body, as discussed above, are integral to the ways in which each of these processes functions. While I draw on specific occupations, the analytical framework could be easily applied and adapted to different fields of work.

A Burden of Doubt

Discussing the effect of the simultaneous enactment of visibility and invisibility of black bodies, an analysis which can very easily be stretched to include women, Goldberg states, 'Race hides those it is projected to mark and illuminates those it leaves unmarked' (1997: 80). It is thus the unmarked who are illuminated as able, intelligent and proficient, as having the temperamental qualities of leadership (Dyer 1997: 14). Not being the standard bearers of the universal human, women and non-whites are instead highly visible as deviations from the norm and invisible as the norm. Existing as anomalies in places where they are not the normative figure of authority, their capabilities are viewed suspiciously. Since human characteristics have been historically constructed as gender- and race-specific, they are not imagined as free-floating qualities; rather they are imagined within specific bodies and not others. There is a significant level of doubt concerning their capabilities to measure up to the job. Although they endure all the trials and tribulations involved in becoming a professional, they are still not automatically assumed to have the required competencies. There is a niggling suspicion that they are not quite proper and can't quite cut it. They have thus to prove that they are capable of doing the job. They bear a burden of doubt. The burden may be larger in some sectors and institutions than in others, but it is nevertheless present in some form or another.

The following remarks were made when speaking of the pressures imposed by the burden of doubt that haunts racialised staff in the senior civil service:

> I feel that I have to prove that I am at least two or three times as good as anybody else before I am allowed in.[2]

> As a member of an ethnic minority you have to do much better than everybody else ... you really have to excel.

In order to combat under-expectations racialised minorities have to prove themselves. As they are not automatically expected to have the appropriate competences, they have to make a concerted effort to make themselves visible as proficient and competent, in a place where they are largely invisible as automatically capable. Thus they have to work against their invisibility.

Infantilisation

The reluctance to accept racialised bodies as being capable occupants of senior authoritative positions can result in infantilisation. Fanon (1986) has observed infantilisation as one of the ways in which racism is manifested. People are assumed to have reduced capacities. Placed as minors in a social hierarchy, they are assigned as having lesser faculties. In the occupational world, infantilisation involves women and racialised groups being imagined as much more junior, in rank terms, than they actually are. As the occupant of a senior position is not imagined to be non-white, often a black person who resides in a senior position is seen to be much more junior than he or she actually is and thus overlooked. Within the senior civil service, for instance, infantilisation places these black senior civil servants in scenarios of the following kind:

> I would often phone another grade seven in another department and they would listen to you and ask your name and immediately say talk to my HEO [Higher Executive Officer],[3] which is their junior. But the general assumption is that, because they hear your name, or they see you, is that you must be in a lower grade. That kind of thing happens every day. I mean if I go with one of my staff who is junior to me, but may have even more grey hair than I have, and they don't know me, they will automatically assume that the other person is more senior to me. That happens quite regularly ... either I go and introduce myself and say I am [mentions his title] and introduce my colleague. Whereas you can see their hand approaching for the other one first because they assume he is senior.
>
> I've had occasions when I've gone with a member of my staff to meetings, where people haven't known me and it's automatically assumed that I'm not the senior one, it's the person whose with me. That sort of thing. It's just a perception that people have that the Grade ... whose come to meet me is going to be a white person.

The above incidents offer some sense of how it is automatically assumed that black bodies cannot possibly be capable of occupying senior positions. While they are highly visible as 'space invaders', at the same time they are in many respects invisible. The negative construction of black bodies in the asymmetrical racial binary has placed them outside 'civilised' white places. Thus black bodies in these senior positions are seen as 'different' and the 'unknown', resulting in a series of racialised assumptions. Women are also infantilised, especially when they are young. The process, however, is so much more in evidence on the grounds of race rather than gender, though the burden of doubt is still a pertinent feature of gender in organisations (discussed further in Chapter 5).

Super-surveillance

Not only do these bodies that are out of place have to work harder to convince people that they are capable, but they also almost have to be crystal-clear perfect in their job performances, as any imperfections are easily picked up and amplified. The scholarly work on black bodies, space and surveillance (Keith 1993; Carter, Donald and Squires 1995; Hesse 1997; Fisk, 1998; Sibley 1998) can be extremely useful for analysing the dynamics of surveillance within institutional contexts. In his discussion of the social formation of Los Angeles, Goldberg notes how bodies in 'black' neighbourhoods are continuously under 'Super/Vison': 'the police loom large both in terms of the apparatus of micro-disciplines and as the general form of urban administration and supervision. Helicopters and floodlights ensure the surveilled and supervised visibility of the racially marginalized population within their constructed confines' (1996: 198). Being under super-surveillance, or to borrow Goldberg's phrase 'Super/ Vision', there is a sense in which black men and women are constantly under a spotlight, as they are seen to represent a potential hazard. Existing under the pressures of a microscopic spotlight of racialised and gendered optics, the slightest mistake is likely to be noticed, even exaggerated, and then taken as evidence of authority being misplaced.

Fanon offers an acute observation of the technologies of surveillance that monitor the authority of black bodies to be in professional posts. Here we clearly see how the burden of doubt operates in combination with super-surveillance. He says:

> We had physicians, professors, statesmen. Yes, but something out of the ordinary still clung to such cases. 'We have a Senegalese history teacher. He is quite bright ... Our doctor is colored. He is very gentle.' It was always the Negro teacher, the Negro doctor; brittle as I was becoming, I shivered at the slightest pretext. I knew, for instance, that if the physician made a mistake it would be the end of him and all of those who came after him. What could one expect, after all, from a Negro physician? As long as everything went well, he was praised to the skies, but look out, no nonsense, under any conditions! The

black physician can never be sure how close he is to disgrace. I tell you, I was walled in: No exception was made for my refined manners, or my knowledge of literature, or my understanding of the quantum theory. (1986: 117)

The tenuous position of black professionals is vividly recalled by Fanon. There is a very thin line between being praised and being displaced of authority. The margins for making mistakes are extremely small. The tiniest error in a performance can be picked up and amplified as proof of the person not being quite up to the job. This can be utilised to warrant further surveillance, with observations becoming more and more intensified. A microscopic inspection not only leaves little leeway for inaccuracies, but this inspecting gaze is likely to find what it is desperately searching for. Undue pressure can itself induce mistakes which are indicative of the anxiety and nervousness produced, rather than of the actual abilities of the person under scrutiny.

In our age of 'diversity' the high hopes invested in the appointment of a person of colour as an academic, senior civil servant or politician, for instance, can all too easily be crushed by the smallest errors. These mistakes are less likely to be noted in others, and if they are noted they are less likely to be amplified. Disproportional surveillance finds errors in those who are not absolutely perfect. This in turn justifies further scrutiny, setting in processes of pathologisation.

The visibility of marked bodies, either in terms of gender or race or both, and the added scrutiny ('Super/Vision') that comes with it requires, as depressingly observed by Fanon, self-surveillance and acute astuteness.

Burden of Representation

Due to the existence of a racialised form of surveillance, there is also a racialised reason for wanting to succeed. Knowing that they are in a precarious situation and that the most minor of mistakes could be taken as evidence of incompetence, women and racialised minorities carry what might be termed the 'burden of representation', as they are seen to represent the capacities of groups for which they are marked and visible *per se*. Fanon observed (see above) how there was more than an individual career hanging on the 'Negro' physician's performance. Being seen as representing the capacities of certain racialised groups, there is a consequent burden attached to being one of a minority, as people feel the pressure to do the job well, in order to show that non-white people can also do the work. As one senior civil servant remarked: 'I don't want to do badly. It's partly to do with letting the side down. I'm determined to do well partly because I want to prove to a lot of people that Asian people can do this too actually.'

The pressure to show they can perform, in the face of contrary suspicions, becomes even more pressing when the appointment has been made amidst competing factions, with some vying for the candidate and others being violently opposed to them. For those who have had to fight explicit bias to reach a senior level, the burden of representation is further heightened. A black civil servant mentioned that he found it 'difficult at the beginning' of his present post because another white colleague had 'competed for the job and every one expected him to get it, and they didn't like it when it was given to me'. Given these circumstances, he 'felt a bit under pressure' to win people over by proving that he could do the job and 'do the job better'. From this example, we can see how he was viewed especially suspiciously when he managed to get a position informally 'reserved' for another colleague. Under these negative and conflictual conditions, 'black' staff exist under the spotlight of intense racialised optics.

The Generalists: the Intangibles

Intangible qualities are attached to positions of leadership. These are rarely stated in job descriptions but they none the less remain crucial for the ways in which people are sized up for promotion and organisational honours. An assessment of character is often the most important, though unstated, criterion for selection. It outweighs strictly technical requirements and is so often the deciding factor in the allocation of positions. To those on the outside of selection processes, the judgements can remain something of a mystery. In the senior civil service there is a hierarchical distinction between the more generalist-orientated administrators and the specialists. 'Black' staff are more likely to be employed in specialist posts (lawyers, scientists, economists, statisticians) and are much less likely to be in those positions which assume the skills of a generalist (having sound judgement and general managerial and leadership skills), which are the more reputable posts requiring 'universal' leadership skills. A sense of 'balance', 'maturity' and being 'solid' are all rather vague terms on which 'sound judgement' is based.

In order to throw light on the shadowy phenomena of 'fit', character and institutional endorsement, an example from Edward Said's educational experiences in the United States can help us to consider what some of the unstated 'core' qualities of leadership might be. Although he was academically successful, he wasn't given honorary endowments or positions of status. He had a sense that he did not have the vital ingredients.[4] He observes:

> I did well enough in my Massachusetts boarding-school, achieving the rank of either first or second in a class of about a hundred and sixty. But I was also found to be morally wanting, as if there was something mysteriously not-quite-right about me. When I graduated, for instance, the rank of valedictorian or salutatorian was withheld from me on the grounds that I was not fit for the honor – a moral judgement which I have ever since found difficult to either understand or to forgive. (2000: 559)

> I was not a leader, nor a good citizen, nor pious, nor just all-round acceptable. I realized I was to remain the outsider, no matter what I did. (1999: 248)

Representing the Universal

Who can represent universally is defined in the shadow of the nation and modernity as it has come to be dominantly defined.

Black bodies in professions that pertain to the universal, the general and the truth are, unlike white bodies, perceived to be representatives of their race. This is a phenomenon that can be observed across different fields (Puwar 2004b). It is, though, probably most clearly shown in the world of formal political representation.

Political authority is seen to be appropriate for those who are racially unmarked, and yet black bodies are perceived to be over-determined by race in terms of whom and what they represent. This conundrum necessitates that we remind ourselves of the two cherubs at the beginning of this chapter, which, as noted by Mercer, enact the sentimental trope that ebony and ivory get together in perfect harmony but on closer examination reveal that it is the white cherub who is positioned as the universal human from which the other is differentiated (1995: 25).

Although black and white MPs sit on the same benches as fellow comrades, it is the white MP who is positioned as the 'real' representative of the universal human, not the black MPs. The representative Chamber is defined as a place where MPs air the particular interests of constituents. These particular interests are then rationalised, distanced and separated through rituals and practices of parliamentary reasoning. And, finally, it is the 'greater good', the 'general will' and the 'public good' that prevails. This is the dominant representation of parliamentary democracy. Just as certain discussions see this representation as a 'sham' and a 'myth' (Marx 1843), it is also built on a racial mythology. Not only do we have an institutional representation which mythologises the place as enshrining the 'general will' or the 'public interest', but the bearers and carriers of the national interest are imagined to be white. It is white bodies who are defined as capable of being trusted with the national interest. It is these bodies who are deemed capable of engaging in arduous reasoning to arrive at a point where they can represent the interests of all humans. In contrast, black bodies are not viewed as being the representatives of the human race *per se*. Being the visible carriers of race, they are always considered to be marked by their race, and thus bounded by their race.

Dyer's observation that, if you are unmarked by race and considered to be just human, then you can, unlike racialised people, who are limited to speaking for their race, claim to speak for the whole of humanity (1997: 2) is highly appropriate to the experience of black MPs. Whilst white MPs can just assume that they are seen as universal MPs, black MPs have to consciously assert their ability to represent humanity *per se*. This means that they have to continually work against their designated particularity. The struggle involved in upholding one's ability to be a British MP, rather than an MP who is wholly marked by his/her race, is captured in the following quote from one of the MPs:

> It is important to make clear that you are a British MP, because you know people try to turn you into all sorts of things ... they turn you into a community leader. [You have to struggle] to establish that you're a properly elected MP. Even though they know, they try to make out that you are a black leader ... I make it quite clear that I am a Member of Parliament and I am a British Member of Parliament.

The dissonance between being black and being a 'British' MP results from two social dynamics, which are in fact two sides of the same coin. First, there is the issue of what is Britishness. The British nation is imagined to be authentically white (Rich 1989; Samuel 1989; Anderson 1991; Schwarz 1996). Moreover, the representatives of the British nation are definitely imagined to be white. Indeed, it is probably a little too much to expect black bodies to be considered as representatives of Britishness when the psychic assumption is that, in the words of Paul Gilroy (1987), 'There ain't no black in the Union Jack.' Secondly, we have the phenomena of racial visibility and invisibility (discussed above in relation to the question of authority), whereby whiteness is invisible and blackness is super-visible, to the extent that a black body is always racially particularised. Black MPs are differentiated from the other MPs because of their racial inscription.

Even though black MPs represent a mixed group of constituents, there is still a tendency to see them as only representing black people. Thus everything they do in the public sphere is reduced to their racial identity. White MPs, however, do not have this restriction imposed on them, as they are, as Goldberg says, 'the ghosts of modernity' (1997: 83). Positioned as being over-determined by race, in an institutional position that requires one to connect with constituents from differing social backgrounds (in terms of class, race, gender, etc.), black MPs are in a contradictory state of existence. They are in fact caught in a sisyphean state of existence; even though they toil over the concerns of all sorts of issues and constituents, they are ultimately positioned as representatives of their race rather than representatives of all their constituents. In the following statement we can see how Black MPs have to constantly struggle against the way in which they are positioned: '70 per cent of my constituents are not Asian and therefore it is very, very important that people realise that I act for everybody, and the perception that Asian or black MPs act only for their own people or their own races is just nonsense. I mean all of us ... we act for everybody.'

Representing What?

Not only are black MPs singled out as being marked by their racial particularity in terms of whom they can represent, but also in terms of what they can represent. It is assumed that race is their main interest. Mainstream subjects, like the economy, the environment and so on, are not considered to be their 'natural' domain. So they feel that 'whereas a white MP can choose his special interest, our special interest is foisted upon us'. It is only when black MPs have something to say about race that they are treated seriously. Some of them feel trapped in this 'strait-jacket':

> it's very sad we are in a strait-jacket, and so you think you are totally labelled and you are not really seen as real Members of Parliament anyway, we are seen as real Members of Parliament but as being slightly bizarre. I think it is very difficult for us to be treated seriously on the issues that we want to be treated seriously unless it's race, it is a great tragedy.

Race as a subject marks the black MPs wherever they go. It is always with them, almost as a permanent and automatic topic. Conversely, one could say that white MPs hardly ever have to problematise or discuss their whiteness. Such is the privilege of being racially invisible in a world structured by whiteness (Williams 1997a). We find that black MPs have race as a special interest 'foisted' upon them, whether they want it or not. They have very little choice in this matter. These MPs are predominantly thought of in terms of race and are seen as race specialists. Hence they are over-determined by race. Whilst they may actually want to deal with 'race' issues, they also want the freedom to engage with other more 'mainstream' subjects. It is important to note that the appeal to be allowed to be more than one's race can be heard from black people working in the public sphere in general.

For those who have tried to widen their remit, one of the interviewees noted how it is difficult to avoid being seen as a race specialist, as black MPs are continually pulled and pushed towards specialising in race. This MP observed that black MPs:

> can't hide and run away from the [race] issues. So, whether you like it or not, you will be dragged into a whole number of issues and the press and the media they will be after them on a whole number of issues ... There are some [black MPs] who say they are mainstream MPs and don't want to be sidetracked into race and all these 'black alleys' as they call it. But, whenever something happens on the race front, the press go to them because they are black and that is the difference between them and white people.

It is quite clear from this account how the media, particularly the press, are fixated on the race of the black MPs. The media play a central role in limiting the subject speciality of black MPs to race by constantly focusing on the blackness of these MPs. It is argued that 'the great problem for Black and Asian MPs is the mainstream press, who never see us as anything but Black and Asian MPs'. Interestingly, while they are allocated 'race' as a speciality they are often closely watched for what they say on this nationally sensitive subject. Black MPs have to be especially careful about what they say on race issues, because they know that the media are just waiting and watching them for any kind of controversial statement or behaviour. This leaves these MPs in an apprehensive situation, whereby they place themselves under self-surveillance and try to guard themselves.[5] As one of the MPs said, 'We are so worried about what the *Sun* is going to print about us, and so you know weighing up every word we use on race issues.'

What they say about 'race' occurs in a context in which the media play a key role in enacting super-surveillance upon racialised bodies, especially on those who have jobs that are in the public eye, such as politicians – local, national or international. There is a national phenomenon, as John Solomos and Les Back found in the study of Birmingham City Council, whereby black politicians are associated with 'patronage, criminality and politics' (1995: 101). Black politicians themselves are quite conscious of the fact that they are automatically distrusted: 'People begin with this perception that we must have done something wrong to get where we are today, that we possibly competed unequally, and that there must have been something, some bit of help here, some bending of the rules there.'

Keeping in mind debates on bodies and surveillance, it would not be an overstatement to contend that black MPs similarly exist under conditions of 'Super/Vision'. The media ensure the surveilled, supervised visibility of these black bodies who have stepped outside the confines of their designated spaces. Being under super-surveillance, black MPs are an easy target. As one of them noted, 'I know we [black MPs] are an interesting target, I mean I would be amazed if I wasn't a target and others weren't a target. It's a case that if you put yourself above the parapet you are there to be shot at.' They have to be mindful of what they say on race, as the press are only too quick to brand them as extremists or as unrepresentative of black people's opinions (despite the fact that they have been elected as constituency MPs rather than as black representatives). Black MPs are caught in a double bind: first, they are particularised and constrained to be nothing but race specialists and, secondly, they have to be careful about what they actually say about race. Anything they say that is mildly unconventional, which is easily done in relation to race issues, is very easily labelled as extremist. For instance, as one of the black MPs reflected on her/his own sense of the media watching him/her, s/he mentioned that the media are only too quick to admonish an MP who is nonconformist on race as 'the high priest of race and race hate'. These labels and surveillance techniques just add to the mesh of particularity that black MPs are defined by.

Strait-jacketed

In *Making Myself Visible* the artist Rasheed Araeen (1994) discusses the contortions involved in trying to make himself visible in the institutional world of art, where his work is ethnically marked. He is invited, accepted and appreciated as an artist within tight confines, confines which patronise him and reduce his work to being ethnically specific. Araeen calls upon constitutively exclusive features of modernity, and the place of racialised 'others' within it, to shed greater light on how ethnic marking exists in his profession. Speaking of 'black' artists he says:

> Modernist techniques or methods, including film or video, may be adopted by them. They may even critique the dominant culture (so long as they don't threaten the system). But whatever they do, they must not escape from their specific ethnic or racial identity. For them to adopt an autonomous subject position, like their white contemporaries, would deprive them of the link necessary to authenticise their positions. This is based on the nineteenth century belief ... by which 'others' are ontologically linked to their own cultural roots (African or Asian), and are presumed to be incapable of entering the world of modern ideas without this link. (Araeen 2000: 62)

The participation in modernity of racialised 'others' is thus as marked subjects who can't escape their 'ethnic' identity. The racial particularity they are said to carry is highly visible, while the particularity of whiteness, as pointed out in the discussion above, is invisible. Furthermore, the artwork itself is seen to be, at some point or another, mimetically linked to an ethnic specificity. It is on these limited and narrow terms that recognition is most easily granted.

Thinking about the impact of the process of marking and ethnic reification upon the institutions of art, Eddie Chambers states that there is in operation an administrative logic for regulating and managing cultural difference. For instance, there has, he says, been in evidence an increasing obligation and responsibility for funders to support black artists within institutional notions of multiculturalism, internationalism and cosmopolitanism. However, despite the apparent 'openness' of these initiatives which seek to diversify institutions, he notes that there is a tendency to make 'black slots' available within digestible constrictors of ethnic vibrancy (1999: 27).

We are witnessing an unflagging multicultural hunger within the drive for diversity in institutions. Alongside this shift, long-standing traditions seem to be alive and well, as the spiritual, authentic, exotic, religious, ceremonial, innocent and barbaric (Said 1995) continue to be the dominant ways in which diverse bodies are received. Difference continues to be celebrated but trapped in managerial and reified understandings of multiculturalism. In more bohemian and avant-garde circles, the fascination has moved on from essentialist notions of tradition and culture to the newness of hybrid cosmopolitan bodies (Hall 1998;

Cohen 1999; Puwar 2002, 2003c). The effect of both of them is similar – objectification and fetishism. Easily available tropes such as Bollywood and 'black cool' are preferred over open-ended conversations.

The connection between the body and the reach of ideas remains tight. Even approaches that attempt to 'democratise' public institutions by bypassing experts to bring in hitherto unheard voices find it hard to frame these conversations and representations outside long-standing, and much criticised, dichotomies. A naïve populist empiricism seeks to 'reach out' by continuing to hear through established epistemic categories.

All speech is embodied and spoken from somewhere, but the issue here is that the speech of 'black artists' is mimetically taken back to what their ethnic and cultural positioning is read as being. The struggle to escape the fixity of racial identities, as well as those of gender, sexuality and class, is summed up by the artist Sonia Boyce, when she says:

> Whatever black people do, it is said to be about identity, first and foremost. It becomes a blanket term for everything we do, regardless of what we're doing ... I don't say it should be abandoned, [but] am I only able to talk about who I am? Of course, who I am changes as I get older: it can be a life-long inquiry. But why should I only be allowed to talk about race, gender, sexuality and class? Are we only able to say who we are, and not able to say anything else? If I speak, I speak 'as a' black woman artist or 'as a' black woman or 'as a' black person. I always have to name who I am: I'm constantly being put in that position, required to talk in that place ... never allowed to speak because I speak. (quoted in Mercer 1995: 30)

Boyce's account reveals the strait-jacket of marked identities, which repeatedly attempt to lock the speaking subject outside universal speech and within particular ethnic enclaves.

On several occasions the artist Steve McQueen has publicly commented on the attempt to view his work as something very particular to blackness *per se*, rather than just art. In a conversation with the cultural artist Kobena Mercer at the Institute of Contemporary Arts (ICA) in 2000 in London, he remarked on his time as a student at Goldsmiths College in the 1980s and how he faced this constant expectation that he would want to create something 'ethnic' in the anthropological sense, such as carnival masks, and would not want to engage with what are termed mainstream issues. He has now won the Turner Prize (in 1999) and created numerous projects which are cinematic revelations in themselves. But, still, some people can't desist from wanting to know how his work speaks from the deepest depths of his blackness. At a public discussion of the screening of the gripping journey down a mile-deep mine in South Africa, *Western Deep*, and the lamenting *Caribs Leep*, shown in the concrete cast of the first Cinema Lumière in Leicester Square, a member of the audience asked McQueen how being black affected his artwork. Being no doubt fully conversant with tiring questions which indirectly ask 'What is it like to be the black you?' and 'Please show us where precisely the black is in the works you create?', to this question McQueen shrugged his shoulders with a facial expression which said, 'Isn't that just a ridiculous, predictable question?' (McQueen 2002).

Visibility: Seeking But Not Hearing

In the arts, literature and academia there has been a notable shift in the near invisibility of black texts and cultural production to significant visibility. In fact, some commentators have noted an over-exuberance. Undeniably the migrant, the refugee and the exile are the figures of our time. However, how they are received is questionable. What speaking position is allotted to them and the investments in this figure deserve scrutiny. There is a fascination with seeking out the 'down below' (Puwar 2003a,b). Michael Keith (1999) notes, for instance, that Bangladeshi youth in Brick Lane, a long-standing, run-down, migrant area of East London, are treated by academics on the Left as the teleological delivery boys.

The fascination with whoever becomes defined as the archetypal figure of alterity is found in forums across different sectors. This is an international phenomenon. People are mesmerised by this 'object' of otherness. Speaking of how this notion is embedded in Hoxton in London (UK), a relatively impoverished area which in the 1990s became fashionable with those who ally themselves with new creative-media arts and industries, the renowned novelist Zadie Smith mentions:

> One of the strange things about Hoxton, which is particularly intense there but mirrored throughout the young middle-class university educated people of this country, is a real desire for a story or some kind of victimhood that they don't have. The story you hear most often in the *Hoxton Bar & Grill* or the *Electricity Showroom* is how difficult it is to be white, for your parents to both be academics and have no story of your own. They are constantly looking for ideas for this film or that film, but no one really has a plot. There is a kind of envy of people different from themselves, as if, for example, cultural minority status gives other people immediate access to creativity that the

Hoxton kids think they themselves don't have. Personally, I'm not interested in writing about my own experience for the rest of my life, but it is seen as a gift that I've been given, both class and race, which separates you from this huge, liberal intelligentsia. (Smith and Dodd 2000: 36)

In the world of literary and cultural studies, the swarm of interest for certain female figures, such as Toni Morrison, Zadie Smith or Meena Alexander, is particularly notable. Picking up on the extent of the attention paid to Zora Neale Hurston, Michelle Wallace presents a vivid picture of what we are in the middle of. She notes that there is a 'traffic jam' of intellectuals engaged in the analysis of the work of Hurston, who, 'like groupies descending on Elvis Presley's estate', are engulfed in 'a mostly ill-mannered stampede to have some memento of the black woman' (cited in DuCille 2001: 234).

Speaking of academia, bell hooks notes that the 'courses I teach on black women writers and Third World Literature are overcrowded, with large waiting lists' and the students are mostly white and privileged (1991: 131–2). Shedding further light on how 'minority discourse' has become 'a hot topic' in the West (Chow 1993: 109), Ann DuCille notes the shift from how 'black' women had to struggle to get black feminist texts on the curriculum or the bookshops to a situation where now:

Within and around the modern academy, racial and gender alterity has become a hot commodity that has claimed black women as its principal signifier. I am alternately pleased, puzzled, and perturbed – bewitched, bothered and bewildered – by this, by the alterity that is perpetually thrust upon African-American women, by the production of black women as infinitely deconstructable 'othered' matter … Why are they so interested in me and people like me (metaphorically speaking)? Why have we – black women – become the subjected subjects of so much scholarly investigation, the peasants under the glass of intellectual inquiry in the 1990's? (2001: 234).

Sonia Boyce, Zadie Smith and Ann DuCille pick up on how a very specific speaking subject position is made available for racialised minority women. They are expected to impart words of wisdom about alterity, or, as Smith says, class and race. This is a very particular speaking position; the utterances of these people are linked to their bodily existence. Their voices are anchored to what they are seen to embody. This is a burden and a connection that is not the first consideration that comes to mind when a white male body speaks, writes or creates. He just speaks as a human, because race and gender are ex-nominated from his bodily representation. While we can no doubt show how this universal figure of a human, who is commonly assumed to be speaking from nowhere is speaking from somewhere, as an embodied being (in terms of nationality, gender and class, for instance), he nevertheless occupies a position of privilege of invisibility.

The visibility of black women is thus of a very specific sort. Their contributions are sought and illuminated, but in limited ways which circumscribe what they have the authority to speak of. They are offered the floor to speak of marginality. The invitations are thus coming in today, but so often they are to fill specific 'ethnic slots'. One enters as a racially marked speaker. As space is opened up, in the same gesture it is closed down under the rubric of a strait-jacket. Taking a critical look at the terms in which one is able to speak within academia, Spivak has noted the existence of a kind of 'benevolent imperialism' that enables her to speak as an Indian woman today. She notes that 'A hundred years ago it was impossible for me to speak, for the precise reason that makes it only too possible for me to speak in certain circles now' (cited in Landry and Maclean 1995: 194). She is invited to speak almost as a gesture of charity and guilt; organisations want to make room for women of the third world – only, however, as specific types of speaking subjects.

The restricted grounds from which women of colour within academia are enabled to speak can become especially apparent when they go outside the remit of 'benevolent multiculturalism' and write about mainstream subjects that occupy a central place in the academic hierarchy of knowledge. This more generalised form of speaking becomes particularly problematic if the idioms one uses are a touch unconventional. Spivak situates the highly publicised critique of her book *A Critique of Postcolonial Reason* (1999) by Terry Eagleton as being directed from a position that is uncomfortable with the fact that the texts she engages with 'are not confined to Third World women and yet I don't write like Habermas in drag' (Spivak 2001: 21). In other words, she speaks of culture, power and literature (mainstream subjects) without becoming a clone of the white male speaking/somatic norm in academia. She argues that her presence in academia is troubling because:

> I am a woman and as it happens a woman of colour who does not remain confined to the modes of discourse that she is allowed to engage in – speaking about women and speaking about Third World women and speaking about our victimage. That's fine. If a person such as me de-anthropologises herself and reads the great texts of European tradition in a way that does not resemble the general rational expectations way of reading then she is punished. (2001: 22)

Whom and what people can speak for is a revealing measure of hierarchies of inclusion. Spivak is steeped in European philosophy and literature, she translated Derrida's tome *Grammatology* in her mid-twenties, and still attempts are made to bludgeon her into speaking about 'her sort' and specific corners of the world. Within the writing of social and political theory, the white man rules, he is still central. Within feminist theory, the white divas have a monopoly over its oration. Women of colour struggle to get into this central ground. They are certainly invited to speak but the queen bees of feminist theory remain white. Structures of whiteness pervade academic and political relations. They have a huge bearing upon who has the authority to speak and in what capacity. There are normative figures who manage to escape racial marking and can thus speak generally, even while they don't escape gendered marking. Their racialised particularity, however, remains invisible precisely because it is the norm. For the woman of colour, as Spivak found, the slot that is made easily available for her is one where she offers herself as an anthropological spectacle. There is a vast open space from where social documentation of oneself or the so-called communities one comes from can be provided. The room for self-commentary is especially forthcoming when the testimonies are able to induce pity, tears or, more recently, a celebration of diversity.[6] There is a particular propensity towards hearing *her* speech from this selective vantage point in all fields, whether politics, literature, academia or the arts.

There are clear parallels between academia, other professions and the art world, where 'black slots' are made available in what Eddie Chambers has referred to as 'the logic of closure, exclusion and guarded tolerance inscribed in arts institutions and the gallery circuit' (1999: 6). In Chapter 3, it was noted how Lévi-Strauss was totally at a loss when he found an 'Indian' sitting in New York library with a Parker pen in his hand. The disorientation he suffered at seeing a member of a group that had been the subject of his academic fieldwork out of the field, so to speak, and now sitting in a place of knowledge, from where the white, Western scholar has looked at and studied 'Other' cultures, was, as noted by Rey Chow, a case of the natives not staying in their frames. That is, the categories through which Lévi-Strauss had seen and located the 'natives' he studied were burst apart by the sheer presence of the 'alien' figure in the library. Chow goes on to note that today, within the academy, scholars from countries outside Europe and North America are specifically sought by faculties, especially within the discipline(s) of Area Studies in the US. She comments on the dynamics of the selection process, by reflecting on a faculty research committee that she was participating in at the University of Minnesota, in the recruitment of a specialist in Chinese language and literature. It is not often academics, or in fact other professionals, risk being branded as renegades (Bourdieu 2001), by going public with what is discussed, behind the scenes, during the course of a recruitment process. Chow offers a rare glimpse of what goes on behind the doors of the selection procedure. For this reason it is worth quoting her observations at length:

A candidate from the People's Republic of China [PRC] gave a talk that discussed why we still enjoy reading the eighteenth-century classic *The Dream of the Red Chamber*. The talk was a theoretical demonstration of how no particular interpretation of this book could exhaust the possibilities of reading. During the search committee's discussion of the various candidates afterward, one faculty member, an American Marxist, voiced his disparaging view of this particular candidate in the following way: 'The talk was not about why we still enjoy reading *The Dream of the Red Chamber*. She does because she likes capitalism!'

This colleague of mine stunned me with a kind of discrimination that has yet to be given its proper name [...] Communist beliefs became the stereotype with which my colleague was reading this candidate. The fact that she did not speak from such beliefs but instead from an understanding of the text's irreducible plurality (an understanding he equated with 'capitalism') greatly disturbed him; his lament was that this candidate had betrayed our expectation of what Communist 'ethnic specimens' ought to be.

[...] In the case of the faculty search at Minnesota, what I heard was not the usual desire to *archaize* the modern Chinese person but rather a valorizing, on the part of the Western Critic, of the official political and cultural difference of the PRC as the designator of the candidate's supposed 'authenticity.' If a native espouses capitalism, then she has already been corrupted. An ethnic specimen that was not pure was not of use to him. (1993: 27–8)

Here we see how employees are called upon to be 'ethnic' in very specific ways, ways which do not in a straightforward way come out of the anthropological archive, but are rather intermeshed with other schools of thought. In this case the anthropological is interwoven with certain versions of Marxism, and its vision of what the subaltern is, or rather should be. When they don't fit into reified notions of the ideal type, they evoke deep disappointment.

Today it is not unusual to see the 'native' sitting in libraries, writing with Parker pens and making public speeches. However, on what subject s/he is expected to carry authority is still coupled with the specific signature s/he is encouraged to bear. There are racialised genres and conventions which effect the ways in which people are heard – self-testimonies, Third World and urban revolutionary zeal, anthropological details and community representation. These slots (speaking positions) are much more easily available to them than the position of the 'mainstream' (universal), which is a position they constantly have to struggle to enter. And in fact when they do they are much more acceptable if they tone down their concerns and speak/mimic the accepted legitimate language in these circles (see Chapters 6 and 7). But even if they are willingly or unwittingly social clones they will always be dogged by the burden of doubt and the tendency of infantilisation. After all, their racial particularity vies with the empty universality of whiteness upon which the position of speaking for everyone is premised. Reflecting on being a black academic in Britain, Felly Nkweto Simmonds notes, 'In the final analysis, I might be an academic, but what I carry is an embodied self that is at odds with expectations of who an academic is' (1997: 228).

Performative Rites: Ill-fitting Suits

the political lion skin has a large mane and belonged to a male lion; it is a costume for men. When women finally win the right to don the lion skin it is exceedingly ill-fitting and therefore unbecoming.

Pateman, *The Disorder of Women*

you feel very sort of, very much like an outsider, because it is such a male institution, because it is an institution built by men, shaped by men, in men's image you feel sort of separate from it and you think you're not part of it and it's quite difficult to get into your stride.

Female Labour Party MP

you learn the style, and the norm is the male style.

Female Labour Party MP

The Body At Work

The body has come to occupy a central place in discussions of gender, most particularly in relation to questions of subjectivity, power and identity. Attention to the ways in which bodies are being altered, in new forms of media or through actual cuts, extensions and insertions into physical bodies, is a topic that has generated increasing interest among academics and social commentators. Within the well-established area of work and employment, while it is standard practice to discuss labour power as a commodity, the body remains a benign rather than consciously theorised entity. Disciplinary fissures between what has come to be caricatured as the hard-core, morally right, area of labour studies and the post-modern, frivolous locale of representation and subversion have to some extent kept apart questions of bodily performance from those of institutions and work. It has become *de rigueur* in studies of employment to observe gendered dynamics by plotting vertical and horizontal forms of segregation across and within organisations (Crompton and Sanderson

1990). But attention to posture, comportment, dress, etiquette and speech is a methodological practice that is not regular research procedure in studies of work and employment, even though there is a very rich and suggestive literature on affective labour (Hardt and Negri 2000; Hochschild 2003; Witz, Warhurst and Nickson 2003).

Those researchers who work at the intersections of cultural studies and gender, work and organisations have certainly taken the body into consideration in the construction of masculinities and femininities in the workplace (Wolkowitz 2001; Nixon 2003). Nevertheless the body has not yet taken root in standard theories and methods of labour studies. An overarching dichotomy in the field of social theory between cultural and economic modes of analysis goes some way towards explaining the gaps in interdisciplinary conversations (discussed further in Barrett 1997; Kellner 1997).

If we want to shed some light on the question of what happens when women and other groups who have been traditionally excluded from specific parts of the public sphere eventually enter them, the body can't be left out. In order to interrogate the conceptual basis on which women and other marginalised groups enter spaces previously closed to them, we are drawn to the ways in which bodies have been coupled with and decoupled from specific occupational spaces.

When Pateman says (1995: 6) that the political lion skin is a costume for men and that it is exceedingly ill-fitting and unbecoming for women, she is making an explicit link between the political realm and the (unspoken) body. The long history in Western social and political thought where women have been the other of the unstated (male) norm has inflected the terms upon which women can today reside in the body politic. The female body is an awkward and conspicuous form in relation to the (masculine) somatic norm. This is precisely why for women the political costume is (a): ill-fitting; and (b) unbecoming. A sedimented relationship between the masculine body and the body politic has developed. This historical link between specific sorts of social bodies and institutional positions is, though, at the same time a performative accomplishment that requires constant repetition in order to be reproduced (Butler 1989). Hence it is open to change and variation – usually, though, within limits.

A Convergence of Gender/Occupational Scripts

The histories of our positions of leadership within the public realm have been such that we have witnessed the convergence of gendered and occupational scripts. The separation of spheres into public and private and the splitting of human bodies into male and female mean that there has emerged a gendered symbolism in regard to positions of leadership (Reskin and Padavic 1994; Gherardi 1995). Power, authority, rationality and the public have historically been associated with an undeclared masculine figure.

By asserting the coupling of gender/occupational scripts, we need to be alert to not operate with a model of analysis based on an additive dual-systems theory which relies on an 'add women and stir' style of theorising. In a critique of the additive use of the term patriarchy with class, Joan Acker (1989) has asserted the importance of the concept of intersectionality, which should not see analytical structures independently with links between them, but rather see how linkages are inbuilt from the start. So, when, for instance, we analyse the body politic, instead of locating gender and the role of MPs in two independent structures (legislatures and gender), we need to think of them as being inbuilt. Both of these scripts are fused. Genders are simultaneously produced and re-enacted through the rituals within the higher echelons of the body politic – as they are in other organisations (see Acker 1990). Thus the routine ritualistic enactment of the script of an MP simultaneously involves the repetition of gendered scripts. The two are interwoven together, and the body is central to the way in which they are synchronised.

Theorising Performative Gendered Scripts

Occupational scripts are, like all forms of masculinity and femininity, 'animated' (Butler 1996: 111) by the body. This is a dynamic process. The work of Judith Butler is most commonly associated with gender and performativity but it is rarely applied to studies of work (McDowell 1997). One of the reasons for this is no doubt the disciplinary fissure mentioned earlier. However, some of this also has to do with a common misreading of Butler's theoretical framework – a reading that she herself is fully aware of and has responded to (Butler 1996: 111). A voluntarist reading of her text *Gender Trouble* (1989), to which her subsequent books *Bodies that Matter* (1993a) and *Excitable Speech* (1997a) partly attended to, has overemphasised notions of play and the subversive power of parody, especially in relation to drag. Both supporters and critics have overlooked the place of the restrictive in her theory, in terms of sedimented ideals and conventions. This misrepresentation might partly explain the lack of engagement with Butler's understanding of the performative in employment studies where researchers seek to highlight the limits of work situations. For an analysis of how structure and agency both impinge upon how gender is done and redone through bodily re-enactments, I have found her reflections to be extremely productive when applied to institutions.

Butler starts from the premise that there is no essential essence to gender, gender is not a fact, gender is something one is always in the process of becoming. Thus our gendered identities do not express our so-called natural gender, because after all there is no such thing, but rather our gendered identities are a performative accomplishment. Using a theatrical analogy to explain the construction, reproduction and trans-formation of genders, she contends that gender is not 'a role which either expresses or disguises an interior "self"' rather gender is an act (1997b: 412). This means that we do not have gendered identities prior to the performance, they are constituted through that performance. We become gendered bodies 'through a series of acts which are renewed, revised, and consolidated through time' (1997b: 406). Although these gendered acts are not natural, in the sense of being expressive of some inner self, continuous repetition of these acts over time, often years, makes them appear natural, giving us the 'illusion of an abiding gendered self' amounting to a set of 'cultural fictions' of what is a real man or a real woman (1997b: 402).

The force of these cultural fictions should not be underestimated. They result in what Butler refers to as 'the deeply entrenched or sedimented expectations of gendered existence' (1997b: 407). She points out that 'certain kinds of acts are usually interpreted as expressive of a gender core or identity' (1997b: 411) Seeing gender as 'an identity tenuously constituted in time – an identity instituted through a stylized repetition of acts', she is mindful of how these acts are structured, as she notes that they are a 'performative accomplishment compelled by social sanction and taboo' (1997b: 402). Bringing the theatrical analogy to the fore in her understanding of sedimented gendered acts, she says, 'Just as a script may be enacted in various ways, and just as the play requires both text and interpretation, so the gendered body acts its part in a culturally restricted corporeal space and enacts interpretations within the confines of already existing directives' (1997b: 410).

Whilst Butler emphasises the force of directive norms in the repeti-tion of gender acts, she also stresses that these norms are not fixed and determinate. Because the structural reproduction of these directives requires them to be ritualistically repeated by individuals, it is this very requirement that leaves the space open for their disruption, for 'the possibility of a different sort of repeating, in the breaking or subversive repetition of that style' (1997b: 407). Holding both structure and agency together in her analysis of gendered acts, Butler asserts that:

> The act that one does, the act that one performs, is, in a sense, an act that has been going on before one arrived on the scene. Hence gender is an act which has been rehearsed, much as the script survives the particular actors who make use of it, but which requires individual actors in order to be actualized and reproduced as reality once again. The complex components that go into the act must be distinguished in order to understand the kind of acting in concert and acting in accord which acting one's gender invariably is. (1997b: 409)

If we take a cue from this framework, it is possible to consider the kind of gendered scripts (styles, acts, performances) – the 'kind of acting in concert and acting in accord' – has been forged into the script of a gender/MP as bearing specific forms of masculine accomplishments. The sedimented styles of bonding, social organisation and bodily enactment place women MPs in a position full of paradoxes and contradictions. Butler's theoretical framework could, of course, be applied and amended to any study of gender, work and organisation – an analytical strategy that has been surprisingly under-utilised. I am offering one particular case-study of this intellectual exercise. The same methodological and theoretical tools could be utilised for understanding how gender is embedded in the structures, processes and daily practices of other institutions. Different fraternities no doubt generate specific 'gender regimes' (Connell 1987). While the body sits right in the middle of all of these, it is, however, little explored.

A Violent Performance

Accepting that 'style is never fully self-styled, for living styles have a history, and that history conditions and limits its possibilities' (Butler 1997b: 40), the performative style of an occupational position has to be placed in historical context. Connell's analysis of changing hegemonic masculinities can be of great assistance for understanding the different configurations of male styles of power and leadership. Taking a historical view of the masculinised image of the body politic, he notes that the:

> Gentry masculinity was closely integrated with the state. The gentry provided local administration (through justices of the peace, in the British system) and

staffed the military apparatus. The gentry provided army and navy officers, and often recruited the rank and file themselves. At the intersection between this direct involvement in violence and the ethic of family honour was the institution of the duel. Willingness to face an opponent in a potentially lethal one-to-one combat was a key test of gentry masculinity, and it was affronts to honour that provoked such confrontations. In this sense the masculinity of the gentry was emphatic and violent. (1995: 190)

There have been notable shifts in the forms of masculinity that have congregated in Parliament over time. With the transition from feudalism to capitalism and the extension of the franchise to all men and women, the composition of the members changed (Stanworth and Giddens 1974; Putnam 1976; Wakeford and Urry 1973; Scott 1991). The ascendancy of the gentry waned, as men from other classes occupied Parliamentary seats (Guttsman 1963). The nature and form of the transition to bourgeois democracy did not involve a clean break with the aristocracy (Scott 1990). Historically the aristocratic form of masculinity, organised around direct domination, has been challenged by a masculinity that conversely values rationality and technical knowledge (Seidler 1989; Hearn 1992). In Britain the 'lengthy osmosis between agrarian capital and industrial development' (Chambers 1994: 19) has meant that both forms of masculinity currently exist and inflect each other within the state. And this is even the case today when the 'professional classes' predominate in the House of Commons (Burch and Moran 1985).

Parliament, for instance, is the place where the feuding gentry have undertaken the symbolic gesture of putting their arms to rest, with the two opposing sides of the House literally being two sword lengths and a foot apart, for the voice of reason. However, while physical violence is replaced by rational verbal communication in the formation of the bourgeois state, the combination of violence, sexuality and political power remains in the rituals (Pitkin 1984; Brown 1988, 1995), only now it is bureaucratically/theatrically institutionalised. In a moment we shall see how lethal one-to-one combat has continued to play a central part in the parliamentary performance; and, while violence is displayed to excess in the theatrical delivery of violence in the Chamber, it is also apparent in other more subdued arenas of professional life, where it is bureaucratically activated (Franzway, Court and Connell 1989).

In spite of the bourgeois representation of political debate as being all about disembodied reason and outside bodily and affective particularity, theorists of embodiment, particularly feminists, have argued that the body and affectivity are actually integral to political speech and debate. Joan

Landes reminds us that 'style and decorum are not incidental traits but constitutive features of the way in which embodied, speaking subjects establish claims of the universal in politics' (1998: 144). The speech, voices, styles and decorum of the bodies that utter parliamentary speech are heavily masculinised. And, in fact, the bodily gestures, movements and enactments reveal strong traces of gentrified heroic masculinity. Despite the claims of bourgeois rationality, aggression continues to play a huge role in the performance of public debate. One could see the Chamber as a theatre where displays of aggression are, as one MP put it, 'cloaked in fine sounding words' for a spectatorial public performance (see Huet 1982). The two swords' length and a foot apart architectural structure of the Chamber is itself combative (interestingly, there is still a rifle-range in the House). Furthermore, it is a theatricalised public sphere scripted for male performances. Tough, ruthless, aggressive behaviour is admired. Those who are able to humiliate their opponents through highly articulate performances which re-enact the violence and theatrical force found in the law courts are especially applauded.

Performances in the Chamber were characterised by a number of the women MPs that I interviewed as being predominantly adversarial, aggressive and 'macho'. In their words it is seen to be an 'individualistic' environment with men performing 'this sort of ridiculous point scoring across the Chamber'. Most of the women MPs see the Chamber as a theatre of 'hostility' and 'pettiness', with a lot of time wasted on unnecessary 'argy-bargy'. These verbal displays are articulated as being 'pointlessly aggressive'. Debate is 'cut and thrust ... Even the cut and thrust of debate is quite a revealing phrase, you know, as if it was a battle.' Aggressive gestures, postures and movements accompany verbal displays. The whole body is propelled into this performance, where finger-pointing, the stern folding of the arms, hands on hips and the thrusting of chests are all called upon. Such masculine bodily displays of aggression are, of course, not confined to the House of Commons; they can also be found in other male arenas (Roper 1993; McDowell 1997).

Prime minister's question time is seen to be particularly prone to a 'yah booh Billy Bunter' style, full of 'boorish noisy nonsense' where winning and losing are spectacularly played out, almost to excess. After all, 'you're not a serious politician, if you can't point score and be abusive and shout and bore at prime minister's question time'. In accompaniment to baritone sounds of 'hear! hear!' order-papers are slapped on the wooden bench in front, feet are stamped, fingers are pointed, brows are tightened, arms are crossed and laughter is roared. The ability to fuse humour with a combative stance is especially applauded, and humour itself is gendered.

Because there is a shared interest in football amongst a large element of the male fraternity, if 'you can make a decent sort of football statement, that wins you a lot of Brownie points' (Female Labour MP).

Fraternal Cathexis

Competitive displays of heroic masculinity are combined with a territorial, hierarchical and deferential form of fraternal cathexis. This interesting psychic mixture was characterised by a woman in the Conservative Party as constituting a 'gang-like' mentality. It underscores the part of politics that is rooted in wars, gangs and leagues that have an intensely homosocial nature (Gasset 1961). Thus it is important to emphasise that there are different and competing fraternities in the House. The cathexis that is forged overlaps with fraternities in other male-dominated places. There are significant party differences in terms of social associations. The male clubs on Pall Mall are largely seen as being an upper-class masculine phenomenon of the Conservative Party. The drinks, food, furniture, décor and stately male ambience of these clubs closely resemble the milieu of the House of Commons. Fraternities within the Labour Party are still more likely to be connected with football, trade unions, working men's associations and local authorities (Labour Research 1997).

Parliament is a monument whose architectural and theatrical style of embodiment is mirrored across a network of space, such as the debating chambers in Oxbridge and public schools. Together these institutional spaces form a physical, social and psychic web of 'archi-textures' (Lefebvre 2002: 118). If we accept that the body has a memory, for those MPs who have moved in these interconnected webs of spaces, the performative movement of their arms, legs, chests and shoulders within Parliament bears memories which take them back to the intimately familiar. Keeping in mind Butler's reflections on gender acts, we could say these acts are part of a series of gender/MP acts that are renewed, revised and consolidated through time and across space, amounting to a legacy of sedimented acts. There is an interpenetration and superimposition of bodily acts from interwoven social spaces. Furthermore, social relations and networks forged in these places are carried over into Parliament as they are into élite positions in other occupations. Thus for some MPs they are putting their theatrical performances into action amongst their peers. The 'social capital' they bear is part and parcel of their social activities. In a very real sense this means that we have scenarios where 'Our Party is very imbued with public school and Oxbridge and all that

– "That's how it is old boy, that's how we do things'" (Gillian Shephard cited in McDougall 1998: 50).

> I think you even see it in the Scott report where so many of ... the ministers concerned were part of it, who had often been to the same school and the same college and so on. It's really hard for anybody outside of that to imagine that. I mean I just cannot imagine coming in here sitting on the front bench and finding ten people from my grammar school on the bench beside me ... They are with people they have been with since they were five years old. (Female Labour MP)

Having an overwhelming majority of male members, who bring with them a range of interconnected, largely fraternal, associations, contributes to the clubbish nature of the House. As men move between various male spaces, creating layers upon layers of overlapping networks, an 'all boys together' atmosphere is forged, which builds on familiar forms of cathexis. Within such a system, members achieve respect through displays of oratory violence towards opponents, but they obtain supporters by affirming their 'brothers' through displays of deference in the Chamber. These are the gang-like terms of promotion. Commenting on the display of deference in the Chamber, MPs said:

> The other day one of the longest speeches was a sort of piano praise from the Member of Isle of Wight to the newly appointed Governor for the Isle of Wight. Now you know there is brown-nosing and there is brown-nosing, but this was ridiculous. (Female Labour MP)

> In this place, you don't make progress by disagreeing ... You must realise that these men will stand up and eat crow publicly to get a knighthood, because now and for the rest of their lives they are going to have the status of being called Humphrey do dar. It's very corrupting. (Female Conservative MP)

Subservience and aggression are together built into the rules and rituals of Parliament. Those who don't follow them can very easily be undermined for speaking out of turn (Shaw 2002).[1] Members are called to speak in the House with preference for those who have served the longest. Ritual and authority are intermeshed with forms of male cathexis carried over from other institutions.

By looking at some aspects of the normative male performance in the Chamber, we have been able to see the costumes men don in the simultaneous performance of gendered identities and the role of an MP. I shall now move on to take a closer look at the entrance of women into this combative, hierarchical, deferential clubbish political theatre.

Violating Visible Bodies

The Chamber is a place where aggressive debates are conducted, with one side of the benches vocally attacking the other. This is the performative norm. There is a display of deference through particular rituals and speech acts. The display of overt conflict across the Chamber may actually be a masquerade that mystifies the level of agreement and convergence in the actual politics of the different parties. What, however, is distinctive about the insertion of women into this violent political theatre is that women's bodies are visible in a way that men's bodies are not. This means that the attack on women MPs can often be mediated through their bodies, with their bodies being used as an additional source of fuel during the exchange of political fire. Women of all political parties mentioned in personal interviews with me that abusive comments about women's bodies are made:

> in a way that no one would ever comment on the men as sort of sexual objects as they are standing up and speaking. I mean it just doesn't cross your mind you know. But the women's sexuality is with them all the time; it's a difference, inappropriately with them. But that's how they look at women. Whereas when a man is getting up and making his speech you don't even think about his body. (Female Labour MP)

The focus on women's bodies exists amongst men of all parties, but it is seen to be particularly acute in the Conservative Party. Speaking of the time when Parliament wasn't televised, a Labour Party MP observed that there was: 'A hooligan element in the Tory backbenchers who made a point of baiting new Labour women. They would often not just tackle what you were saying in a debate, they were making remarks about your clothes, her hair and her make-up. You know all very destructive ... and very disgusting.' The televising of Parliament has, however, calmed down only some of the abusive behaviour. But it is still prevalent, albeit in a subdued form,

> it is a bit more subtle and it's a bit quieter ... there is still a predominant atmosphere like that, that is very yah booh and Billy Bunter and stupid and very very male and quite cruel ... That kind of yah booh side of the Commons is very strong and still makes abusive comments about women. (Female Labour MP)

> people still make sexist remarks ... women are still commented upon in the same fairly simplistic, mindless, coarse terms that you might find in the

football terraces ... men are behaving badly here, just as they are anywhere else. (Female Labour MP)

Maybe this behaviour persists because, as noted by Reskin and Padavic (1994), talk about women in sexual terms amongst men underscores a shared sense of masculinity. Soon after the 1997 general election, when a record number of women were elected, Kali Mountford noted that comments like 'Isn't she a pretty girl!' 'Isn't she a feisty young thing!' 'Hasn't she got nice legs!' were shouted across the Chamber to a woman MP (cited in McDougall 1998: 180).

Some men in the Conservative Party also use gestures and body language to put women off their stride when they speak in the House. Despite the increase in the presence of women MPs in the House in 1997, a female Labour MP reported to the press that 'they put their hands out in from of them, as if they were weighing up melons. There are Tory MPs who do it on a regular basis' (*Independent*, 10 December 1997). A female Conservative MP reported that the men on her side of the House swing in a row from side to side when young women MPs on the opposite benches wearing a skirt cross their legs. In her interview with me she stated, 'I mean you know at this age and stage that's what they were doing and I turned around and you know ticked them off a bit, but they don't take much notice. They giggle like silly schoolboys.' In fact, men have themselves admitted that the bodies of women MPs can be a source of male humour and entertainment while they occupy themselves during long boring hours in the Chamber (noted in Julia Langdon, *Guardian*, 1 May 2001, p. 7).

Although some of the women in the Labour Party found that the 'sexual harassment and catcalling' was largely limited to the Conservative benches, most of them thought that it also existed on the Labour benches, albeit in a diluted form. It was stated that Labour men are 'not sweetness and light themselves', as they too make 'niggly remarks' about Tory women. Cynthia Cockburn in her analysis of men's resistance to sex equality in organisations has noted how sexual humour is a form of male control. She argues that a 'source of disadvantage to women is the heightened heterosexual and sexist culture generated by men within the workplace. In contrast to the exclusion of women by male clubbing, this culture includes women but marginalizes and controls them' (1991: 153). Even compassionate sexual humour can in this environment marginalise. For instance, when Margaret Thatcher first walked into the House of Commons as Leader of the Opposition, her own side yelled greetings like 'Give us a kiss, Maggie' (cited in Nunn 2002: 67). In these situations the professional integrity of women politicians hovers on unsteady ground.

Speaking of Female Bodies

The bodies of women MPs seem to be particularly vulnerable to abusive behaviour if they discuss issues that are explicitly related to sexual politics. When women MPs make political speeches about women's bodies, then the male order can be thrown into absolute mayhem. Feminists have suggested that Western thought, in its dualistic conceptualisation of mind/body, has a deep fear and hatred of the body– somatophobia – and particularly female bodies – gynophobia (Daly 1978; Spelman 1982). One MP noted that she did not find debate in the Chamber particularly difficult as a woman until she introduced women's bodies into the discussions. Then she was 'blasted' by 'some pretty gross behaviour in the House'. The 'gross behaviour' entailed abusive personal comments on the body of the MP. It was fuelled further by similar comments from the press.

The House of Commons is a male space that is certainly not accustomed to giving women's issues serious consideration. So talk of female bodies can create bizarre reactions. 'There were a lot of arguments about cervical cancer screening when we didn't have a screening system, and a lot of them would giggle if you mentioned things like that. Very kind of schoolboy, primitive. If there was anything remotely to do with women and their health or the breasts of women, that finished them off completely' (Clare Short cited in McDougall 1998: 59).

Somatic masculine speech finds it difficult to deal with women's bodies from a perspective that does not exoticise, fetishise or ridicule them. The actual physical arrival of breast-feeding women in the House became a huge issue in 2000 when the MP Julia Drown chose to breast-feed her baby in a committee meeting. The Speaker of the House (Betty Boothroyd) declared it forbidden on the basis that beverages were not allowed in committees. The most archaic of rules and rituals, wrapped up in an apparent language of gender neutrality, can be utilised to differentiate the prescribed from the proscribed. Hence, once again, we see how rituals, working practices and performative genders coalesce in the accomplishment of specific institutional scripts that take specific types of bodies as the norm. In 2002 the new speaker made some mild amendments to the ruling by allowing women to breast-feed in a special room set up for the purpose in the Lady Members' Rooms. But the ban on breast-feeding in the Chamber, committee rooms and the press gallery persists despite attempts by a cohort of women to overturn it.

Embodied Speech: Hearing the 'Other' Sex

Because women represent the social sphere that has been excluded from the state, they often have to struggle to be heard in the Chamber. Their speech is not automatically given as much recognition and space as the men's is. There is not a 'natural' congruence between women's bodies and intellectual technical competence (Burris 1996). And, in fact, the super-exposure of women's bodies could be seen to be a case of what Gatens observes to be a strategy used to silence women. This involves the speaker either being animalised or being reduced to her 'sex'. She states: 'Women who step outside their allotted place in the body politic are frequently abused with terms like harpy, virago, vixen, bitch, shrew; terms that make it clear that if she attempts to speak from the political body, about the political body, her speech is not recognized as human speech' (1996: 24).

Some of the MPs noted various ways in which women's speech is not given as much recognition as that of the men. When the House is pressed for time, the assumption is often made that women 'will naturally give way to a man'. During the course of an MP's speech, it is normal for the opposition to undermine the argument by intervening. This intervention is dependent upon the MP who is holding the floor noticing the other MP – bobbing up and down – and giving way. Some of the women in the Labour Party identified this point as a time when they are likely to be ignored. They mentioned that male MPs are much less likely to give way to a woman. This is especially the case when women's intervention is aimed at widening the terms of the political agenda to include questions of gender. So, just as attacks on women's bodies are much more likely to happen if they discuss specific issues, like abortion, pornography or smear tests, for instance, women's attempts at participation in the debate of the House are also much more likely to be resisted if they try to broaden the framework of traditional parliamentary subjects, such as the budget, to those of gender.

Interestingly, while on the one hand there is a resistance to accepting serious talk of women's bodies and gender in this male space, at the same time the subjects are highly gendered. There has historically been a propensity, which is slowly changing, to allocate women the 'soft' subjects, such as those of the caring fields of education, health, pensions and aid. These 'soft' topics not surprisingly lack the kind of weight that is granted to 'hard' subjects, such as foreign policy, economic or defence matters, which are ranked highly. The latter subjects are viewed as the real, tough, 'hard' subjects. As one Conservative woman MP observed:

the male preoccupation which still exists in this place is with foreign affairs and defence. If there is a debate in this place on the army or foreign affairs, which we only have about twice a year, the place is packed. All the men are jumping up and down. They've all got a view about Botswana, Bosnia and every damn place, Bangladesh, you can think of and they all puff up their chests and they want to let you know how many times they have been there and all the people they know there and stuff like that. You have a debate here on social services and the Chamber is empty practically...

The glass ceiling is undoubtedly moving across as women are slowly granted portfolios in the more mainstream 'hard' subjects, such as the economy, foreign affairs and sport, for instance. However, there is still a propensity for territorial departments, such as those connected with arms and land, to be regarded as being especially 'ill-fitting' for women. Responding to the horizontal segregation in this sector, one MP mused: 'there is a little part of me that would like to think that I might be the first spokeswoman on defence, you know, and just break through that wall ... You would have the military chiefs doing their nut, no doubt [laughter].'

The sex typing of roles means that those who just occupy the softer/ women's subjects are not seen as 'hard' politicians. And, although women, as individuals, may question the very designation of 'caring' subjects as 'soft', they still have to work to get promoted within a structure that devalues 'caring'. This presents women with the dilemma of wanting to work on the so-called women's or 'soft' subjects, but at the same time wanting to be taken seriously as tough politicians. As one Labour MP put it:

> things like nursery provision are seen like sort of soft and not really to do with politics. You know if you are going to be a real politician you are going to have to prove you're tough and talk about the public-sector borrowing requirements. And when there were only very few women in politics, they felt trapped, that they couldn't afford to take up the soft stuff or they would just be seen as a woman and they had to prove that they were politicians, as the men might talk about steel and tax and the public-sector borrowing requirement. So I mean things that are of such importance to the country, like, say, child care, which is very important to families and it's very important to the performance of children, was seen as not really a mainstream political issue.

Another MP mentioned that a possible strategy for dealing with the desire to work with 'women's issues', but at the same time avoid being pigeon-holed and ghettoised into 'soft' subjects was to 'fool them by talking about all the lot'. So, to escape being labelled as the woman who just talks about 'women's issues', some women make a point of taking on so-called 'hard' as well as 'soft subjects'. They do it all.

The Burden of Doubt/Representation

Due to the convergence of gender/occupational scripts, historically, the 'core' qualities of leadership are seen to be 'classically' male. The struggle exists in trying to show that the required qualities can exist in bodies that are not 'classically' expected to embody the relevant competencies. Because women are not expected to have certain abilities, there is always an element of doubt, even if it is temporary, concerning their capability to do the job well. Although the doubt may dissipate as people get to know them and see them doing the job, there is an initial hurdle that women have to overcome. Again, this involves women undertaking the labour of undoing gender perceptions. Women MPs 'have to prove ourselves constantly'. Wherever there is a burden of doubt, there is a burden of representation. Women MPs noted:

> I think that you have always got at the back of your mind that, if you don't do your job well, people will sort of say, 'She's not doing as well because she's a woman.' (Female Labour MP)

> I think there is a responsibility when there are only a few of us to make a good job of what we did because if we didn't people are going to say, 'Look at her, there is no point in having more, you know she's made a mess of it.' And that is the added responsibility and I think it is with other women in other jobs ... people are going to say, you know watch carefully. (Female Conservative MP)

When women are in portfolios considered to be 'classically' male, then the burden of doubt/representation pressures are further intensified. Women feel that they have to be careful of making mistakes, 'because they'd love to say, "Well, you can't do the job, you know, this is not traditional." Some women MPs stressed that, when women are given the opportunity to undertake roles that they are not expected to be in, they 'must excel' to show that they can do non-traditional jobs.

Double-edged Visibility

A minority of women MPs argued that women did not suffer any disadvantages for being women. They argued that in the Chamber, like

-91-

everybody else, women got heckled for 'saying stupid things'. Interestingly, women are seen to have a distinct advantage in the allocation of time and space in parliamentary debates. It is argued that the minority position of women makes women much more visible and therefore they are noticed much more easily. Recollecting the experience of entering the House some years ago when women were an extremely small minority, an interviewee stated: 'We had advantages, because if a woman stood she invariably got called to speak. There were so few of us it was an advantage in many respects ... Oh yes, the Speaker would call a woman more than they would call a man, when there was a small number of us. It doesn't happen now' (female Labour MP). It is argued that, being a minority, 'everybody gets to know you very quickly'. Amongst this sea of men in grey suits, the women are highly visible.

Visibility, however can be a double-edged sword. It is argued that 'people respond to whether you are a woman but very quickly they respond to whether they think you have got something to say and whether you are good at the job and if they do think that then you are listened to ... I think it just takes that bit longer if you are a woman' (female Labour MP). The fact that it takes women 'that bit longer' to be heard and respected must not be dismissed as a minor point. It is enormously revealing of the exclusionary processes at work in the differential allocation of respect and authority to gendered bodies.

The flip side to being noticed and being called to speak is that female MPs are in the spotlight. Because they are out of place, women MPs could be said to be under a form of super-surveillance. If they make any mistakes, they are likely to be picked up. The gaze of the public and other MPs is all too often ready to notice any small error they may make. Though invisible in the sense that they are not automatically seen to be qualified for the post, they are simultaneously in the spotlight. While men are illuminated for what they are imagined to be capable of, women are illuminated for being rare in numbers and for what they might be incapable of. Historical sedimentation has enabled the presence of white men to go unremarked and unnoticed. Thus, as women are highly visible as not quite the norm, any mistakes they make are less likely to be overlooked or pardoned. Their capacity to perform the parts of the organisation that have hitherto been largely played by men is continuously under scrutiny. Those who judge are less likely to be forgiving of women than they are of men. Continuous visibility can be wearing and a hazard that makes the authority of women an especially unsteady condition that can all too easily be in jeopardy: 'Men are just more invisible in this place. They can get away with more' (Ann Campbell MP, cited in McDougall 1998: 50).

As there is less of a margin for mistakes or errors it is stated that the 'average standard of the women in this place is higher than the average standard of the men in this place' (Female Labour MP). Being conspicuous, it is much more difficult for the average woman to be mediocre than it is for the average man: 'women have to be somehow very special or far more capable than a man to actually get into that position and I think that we will have succeeded in getting equality for women when women can be as mediocre as men' (Female Labour MP). This was affirmed by an MP in the Conservative Party, who made the following contradictory statement:

> I don't think there are barriers as such, after all we have had the first woman Prime Minister ... But I do think that to get anywhere as a woman you really do have to be better managed, harder working. You have even got to be more able than a man to get up that ladder ... you've got to be absolutely outstanding.

Doing Mutually Exclusive Scripts

Women are judged for the ways in which they 'do' two diametrically opposed scripts simultaneously. They are judged for how they 'do' their gender as well as for how they 'do' the performance of an MP, which, as we have discussed above, is based on a male norm that constitutes the exclusion of all that women symbolise. So, the question is, how can women combine these conflicting and contradictory roles? There is a great deal of labour involved in 'redoing' male and female scripts. An awful lot of energy is expended by women on managing their femininity in a social position constructed in masculine terms, with a masculine body in mind. Butler has emphasised the possibilities of gender transformation through a different and innovative repeating of sedimented norms. At the same time, though, she does not think that innovation is either easy or without risk.

Subversive repetition of the male/MP style requires energy – energy that the traditional public man does not have to expend because he already has a script that he can do with very few changes. Even though he also has to 'put on' gender within 'punitive and regulatory social conventions' (Butler 1997b: 410), 'daily and incessantly, with anxiety and pleasure' (Butler 1997b: 415), he at least has a range of male clones and costumes that he can choose from. As it is still not the norm for women to be in public positions of authority that are outside familial roles, their choice of clones and costumes is much more problematic, even as they engender new entities.

The sedimented style of being an MP is unsuitable for women because it has been created for a male body, to the exclusion of female bodies. This style has been re-created as an image of a 'public man' who represents truth, objectivity and reason. Women cannot expunge their bodies, as they are seen to be over-determined by their bodies. While men's bodies carry weight and carriage, women's bodies signify all that which is excluded from the upper echelons of the public sphere. In fact, their bodies threaten the order and universality of the public sphere, so that, when they enter the political sphere, the presence of their bodies creates an imaginary collision between normative representations of sexed bodies and the body politic. Being out of place, women MPs have to work out a way of redoing female/MP scripts: 'I mean the buildings, the manner of life wasn't set out for women. So you know our society does not quite see women in this position. So you have to work out how you are going to tackle that and work out what you are going to do about it' (Female Labour MP).

In one sense we could interpret the absence of female/MP scripts as a case of women finding themselves, in Irigaray's words, 'homeless' in the symbolic order (see Whitford 1991: 69). Female bodies are largely absent as MPs in the body politic. Women do not have adequate representations, images and institutions to serve as identificatory supports. This presents women who enter this space with the kind of dilemma faced by Pat Schroeder, who withdrew from the 1987 US presidential candidacy because she could not '"figure out" how to occupy the political sphere without turning over her desires, behaviour and plans to predetermined meanings which were at odds with her own intentions' (Gatens 1996: 26).

The absence of female/MP scripts does not mean that the women MPs are totally free to create a new script for themselves. They have to remould their scripts out from within the confines of gendered social conventions, and this is particularly problematic when they have actually been represented as being counter and thus inferior to the relational definition of the rational, disembodied figure of enlightenment. Since the universal masquerade was specifically made with the male image in mind, women face an enormous struggle when they also try to take part in it.

Managing Femininity

As actors, women MPs are neither totally determined nor in possession of absolute individual choice in the re-enactment of scripts: 'Just as a script may be enacted in various ways, and just as the play requires both text and interpretation, so the gendered body acts its part in a culturally restricted corporeal space and enacts interpretations within the confines of already existing directives (Butler 1997b: 410).

In the House, gender directives are pooled together from different spaces and are often used to label women. As one MP from the Labour Party put it:

> to an extent assumptions are made about all MPs. Both men and women are being eyed up by the ones who have been here for some years. They decide what they think of you, but I think women particularly, you're assessed on how chatty and friendly you are, whether you're thought to be emotional or ambitious or a hard-nosed feminist or whatever. You're quickly labelled.

The risk of being labelled as 'naggers or being thought of as exhibitionists' means that women face all sorts of dilemmas that male MPs rarely have to confront. Under these conditions, women have to weigh up one way of behaving against another. The political issues they articulate are integral to the way they may be labelled. In the words of a Labour woman MP:

> I have continued to keep hold of women's issues as well, because it was tempting to say, 'No I'm not going to do that, so they can't label me as just a woman.' But, on the other hand, I didn't want to be labelled as someone who is denying my femininity. So you know you do have to struggle and think about those things. And I suppose that's what men don't have to do ... What it has meant over my career in terms of political activity is that I've had to work these things out and make decisions about things that my male colleagues have never had to do. So it has been an issue in how I've behaved and the issues I've taken up, all the time.

Women have to manage their femininity in terms of the issues they take up, but also their physical appearance. As the media become more and more important in the making and breaking of MPs, they continue to keep a watchful eye on the bodily image, gestures and postures of the women MPs. As we increasingly enter what Landes calls 'a period where iconic relations on the model of the older "re-presentative" public sphere count for more, stylistically and substantively, than the symbolic, predominantly textual relations promoted by the early bourgeois public sphere' (1998: 156), the media will place even more surveillance on the appearance of women. We have seen how women's bodies matter in the body politic, and the way in which their bodies are always with them.

The media add to and feed into scrutinising women's bodies. Hence the eyes are not only to the left and the right, they are everywhere, and this is the case both inside and outside the House (Norris 1995; Sreberny-Mohammadi and Ross 1996).

In recent times the media image of all MPs has become so important that parties have employed image consultants to package the MPs. In the Labour Party, Barbara Follett and her team became notorious for advising MPs on how to dress their bodies. The hair colour, the size of earrings, make-up, the management of clothing according to the 'science' of colour consultants, the minutest detail of body image are under surveillance. Whilst a significant number of women take this advice on board and find it useful, a few resist it. And, interestingly, the paradox is that the more women achieve or succeed in the hierarchies of organisations the more their look, image, style and size carry significance. Even though men have also been encouraged to take this advice, it is widely accepted that asymmetrical attention is paid to the appearance of male and female MPs. The image of women MPs is observed much more by their peers and the press as well as the public. It is argued that:

> people form impressions about you before you have even opened your mouth. (Female Labour MP)

> people remember what you wore more than what you said on telly. (Female Labour MP)

> I have had the most incredible number of times when people have said 'Oh I saw you on the telly' and I say 'Did you agree with what I was saying' and they have said 'I can't remember what you were saying but that was a nice dress you wore'. I mean some of the men who come on TV you wonder when they last washed their hair, and dandruff on their shoulders. They can get away with that. No woman would dare turn up to a TV studio looking like that. (Female Labour MP)

Coupled with this asymmetrical surveillance, women MPs have the additional problem of a lack of historical precedence. They have a lack of costumes they can don in the acting of a politician's script. Whilst the men have moved from wearing top hats and tails to business suits, women do not have a set style of dress. They have to work at being 'appropriately' dressed, something which has to be negotiated within the confines of gendered norms of dress or what Butler terms 'cultural fictions'. Women MPs do not have to abide by any formal written codes of behaviour concerning dress. Like most codes of behaviour in the House, informal processes sanction codes of dress. They negotiate between unacceptable and acceptable codes: 'You really can't have your skirt hemmed too short. You can't have a neck that is too plunging... So you've got to find that line where you look good, but you're not going over the top' (Female Conservative MP).

Most female MPs draw on popular corporate images of women in positions of power. These images observe feminine codes of behaviour. The House of Commons is a place where binaries are firmly re-enacted in terms of masculine and feminine dress. In this place, men dress as 'men' and women dress as 'women'. The style is acutely differentiated between the sexes. The social fictions of what is considered to be the natural physicality of men and women are firmly entrenched. It is a place where corporeal styles have become sedimented into a binary relationship between reified forms of femininity and masculinity. In these circumstances, many of the women are extremely anxious to 'retain their femininity'. There is thus a tacit collective agreement to perform discrete genders. A 'ladylike feminine' image plays a central role in the struggle to be seen as an acceptable form of 'woman' in a male outfit in a male space.

Fusing Femininity and Masculinity

In relation to the gender acts of women MPs, the scripts are often drawn from other spaces where women have authority, such as the home (nannies), schools (matrons), national monuments (courageous saviours) and even commercial sex (dominatrixes). These have been characterised by Linda McDowell in her study of gender and authority as 'Fearsome models of female authority' (1997: 153). She argues that:

> One of the difficulties for women in male-dominated professional occupations is trying to find an image of a powerful woman, which is not negative. Tannen (1994) suggested a whole menagerie of stereotypical images of women: schoolmarm, headnurse, headmistress, cruel stepmother, dragon, lady, cat-woman, witch, bitch are the only powerful options. To the schoolmarm, nurse and headmistress we might add nanny, matron and governess, all of whom are characters from the youth of the landed gentry and the prep school dormitory. (1997: 152)

Interestingly, Betty Boothroyd has made sense of her style of authority as Speaker of the House precisely in these terms:

I'm something between a schoolmistress and a nanny in this job. Sometimes I do think, is that my voice? Am I so rough? Perhaps I ought to temper myself a little more. I have to stand back and think of that. Am I a bit hard, am I too abrasive? Sometimes I think I'm a little too soft you know, on occasions when I am more tolerant perhaps than I should be. (Cited in McDougall 1998:179)

It is worth noting the ambiguity, uncertainty and self-monitoring attached to Boothroyd's interpretation of herself, veering between too hard and too soft. Alvesson and Due Billing in their expansive and in-depth survey of research for *Understanding Gender and Organization* have noted how the construction of leadership and management positions in masculine terms makes 'it difficult for a female manager to strike a balance between being seen as a competent manager/leader and as sufficiently feminine not to be viewed as breaking with gender expectations' (1997: 91). These dilemmas are, of course, not confined to Parliament; they work across institutions.

Patricia Walters's research on women in the senior civil service, for instance, highlights that there is a perception that women do not measure up to the central core performances (1987: 22). Women, senior positions and the necessary capacities are not imagined to be congruent. They are more likely to be judged, at least initially, as incomplete in some way, and the stretch of their capabilities is seen to be much more limited. The women I interviewed in the senior civil service noted that they had to juggle between being seen as competent and not being too aggressive. They were concerned with doing the job well in an acceptable and feminine way. This balance is difficult to strike when the accepted style and qualities of leadership are embodied as masculine. A woman in the senior civil service remarked: 'Right at the very top level, there are all those sort of intangibles like leadership, figure-head type of person, the authoritative ones, you know, which are often classically seen as male qualities.'

Over time, the male gestures, voices, postures and accents involved in the performance of the role of an MP have been defined as masculine. Therefore, if a woman displays these traits, she runs the risk of being charged with denying her femininity and being masculine. She may be derided for being a ridiculous monstrous aberration on the grounds of women's nature. The cartoon in Figure 6, taken from the *Evening Standard* drawn by David Low in 1929 (Atkinson 1997) mocks the sexist attitude to the whole notion of women sitting in Parliament in skirted suits and hats in bodily postures seen to be exemplary of masculine behaviour. They are shown with their arms folded tightly, their postures slouching and their arms waving. The lived embodiment of

Figure 6 David Low, The Parliament of the Future?, *Evening Standard*, 1929. Copyright permission provided by Atlantic Syndication.

women, as occupying minimal physical space is imploded through the spreading of their bodies in this vast and expansive Chamber. They are not classically demure and 'ladylike'. Thus they are represented in the mind's eye of sexist MPs as well as the electorate as lacking composure, and frankly being a bit of a grotesque joke. This parody of masculine gestures by female bodies clothed in feminine styles of dress, in one reading of Butler's theorisations of gendered subversion, could be seen to denaturalise the fictive nature of gendered norms. In 1929 the parody was used as a derisory method to laugh at old-fashioned attitudes to women in politics. The emphasis is on showing how ridiculous, how unnatural and unfeminine they are seen to look when they try to take on the act of men. This reading of absurdity obviously only works because it is able to capitalise on firmly entrenched notions of how a 'real woman' should look and behave. And, in fact, even today, the utterance 'she's a man' is able to cause pain, precisely because culturally specific core features of femininity are so naturalised.

Dress Like a Lady, Act Like a Man

Margaret Thatcher represents the most famous script of a woman in Parliament. She has provided a widely discussed example of how women may style themselves in a masculine domain. In Margaret Thatcher's particular mix of reified sex-typed characteristics of both masculinity and femininity, she was quite famously labelled as a 'surrogate man', 'the only man in the Cabinet' and the 'iron lady'. She is said to have taken the maxim 'Dress like a lady and act like a man' seriously. When we deconstruct these labels and characters, we can find a whole array of assumptions about the relationship between male and female bodies and masculinity and femininity, as well as the structured masculinisation of institutional positions.

Many of the Labour MPs argued that women are under pressure to act like men in order to be taken seriously. There is a behavioural male norm and women are under assimilative pressures to conform to that norm:

> women are made to behave like men, because those are the structures and you can't get on unless you behave like that... If you are only praised by the men when you behave like them, inevitably you do. (Female Labour MP)

> There are pressures put on you to accept the way men behave and behave in that way yourself. (Female Labour MP)

Judgements and standards are thus measured in relation to this normatively conceived individual. Pateman notes that women have been incorporated into the public sphere as '"women", as subordinates or lesser men' (1995: 14). Women can enter the public sphere as male equivalents. They exchange their role from being not-men to that of like-men. By transgressing spatial boundaries and by entering the public sphere, women do, no doubt, transform and destablise the social order to a certain extent. There is a politics to their sheer presence (Phillips 1998). At the same time, though, women are subject to ambiguous and contradictory interpretations as they are perceived as both a woman and the equivalent of a man.

Similarly, Gatens makes the point that women are granted access to the public sphere so long as they have the 'ability to emulate those powers and capacities that have, in a context of male/masculine privilege, been deemed valuable by that sphere' (1996: 71). Developing this argument further, she states: 'This places those who fall outside this norm in contradictory and conflictual situations, with little opportunity to create a language, or a discourse, in which to voice these contradictions, since the failure to match, or live up to, the norm is understood as a failure of the individual concerned' (1996: 98). The 'cost' of women coexisting in a public sphere that has not been restructured is, symbolically speaking, tantamount to a 'hysterectomy', because women have to erase their difference. Given that women have been associated with the natural as opposed to the rational, or their sex, specifically speaking, their uterus, and that uterus in Greek is *hystera* – hence the English derivative hysteria – Gatens asserts that women can symbolically become prime ministers so long as they become men. Playing on the history of words, she states, 'We can be "cured" of mere animal existence by "becoming men"; "cured" of "hysteria" by "hysterectomy"' (1996: 85).

The pressure to emulate, match up to and live up to the male norm was considered to be particularly strong when women were an absolute minority. As one respondent maintained, 'women had no choice, they had to operate by the men's rules or just be phased out.' Women MPs have interesting opinions on how Thatcher fused being a woman and the Prime Minister. She is said to have behaved like a man by playing the 'boys' game' of shouting in the Chamber, being aggressive and competitive, participating in the drink culture and aligning 'herself as a man on certain issues'. Some MPs stressed that Thatcher was compelled to behave like a man: 'she was a tough politician and the only way she could survive was by being tough... Had she not been tough and determined, (a) she would not have got there and (b) she wouldn't have survived' (Female Conservative MP). Others argued that Margaret Thatcher chose to behave like a male politician while at the same time hailing voters by connecting national economic issues with the everyday concerns of a wife and a mother. She made explicit use of this feminine image through the media:

> She was a mother, she was a wife. She saw herself as a mother with two children. She would go on television and be photographed so she wasn't trying to pretend that she wasn't a mother ... she chose that role as being the only man in the cabinet and all that, she chose that. She didn't have to be like that but that's the role she chose. That was her thing, that was her way of doing it. (Female Labour MP)

It is argued that one of the reasons Thatcher chose to perform gender/ MP in this way was because this was an effective management ploy. She borrowed from other female authority roles (discussed earlier) where women manage men, for managing the men in the Cabinet. Her aggression took a particular gendered form, one that was quite specific to female/male authority dynamics, especially to the experiences of men in the 'high caste Conservative Party', who, as one Conservative MP put it, know women as:

nannies, grannies or fannies ... they know women as nannies, grannies looking after them, housewives if you like and you know fannies. I've said that rather coarsely but it's true and that's how they perceive women. They don't know women as colleagues. They've never worked with them. They've been educated separately from them. Women are kind of exotic creatures that come from another world and they actually are not comfortable with women.

Given that men in the Conservative Party were not used to working with women as MPs, let alone as prime ministers, they were disorientated when they were faced with a woman in what had hitherto been a male outfit. Even if we accept that Thatcher had to behave like a male politician, she could not have been an Identikit male politician because she was in a female body. Being this 'rare species' she could utilise techniques of control from more traditional female authority roles to control the men in her Cabinet. And she may have chosen to only once invite a woman into her Cabinet precisely because women would not have acceded to this form of authority. As one Labour MP put it:

> Margaret Thatcher was very threatened by other women. She knew how to manipulate chaps. But other women saw through that. I mean there is no way that I could feel intimidated by Margaret Thatcher, because I would know what she was up to. She was just being a woman. She was being manipulative and I wouldn't have that and she knows that, and that is why she didn't put women in the Cabinet. I mean a bunch of chaps is much easier to deal with. And I can up to a point see what she was up to.
> [Because] she adopted attitudes in a sense of how women had been taught to manage men, then she had to become tougher than they were. You know she had to become an iron lady.

The 'lady' side of Margaret Thatcher, in terms of her dress, is particularly emphasised by women MPs in the Conservative Party. They stress that she was a tough politician but she wasn't a man. As these MPs have a distaste for women who do not dress feminine, they want to draw attention to the fact that Thatcher dressed like a lady and underplay the fact that she is said to have acted like a man. They argue that 'If she wanted to be mannish she would have been wearing trouser suits and pinstripes, and she obviously didn't. She was very feminine.' Skirts, dresses, pearls and so on are valorised and 'interpreted as expressive of a gender core or identity' (Butler 1997b: 411).

Sexuality also figured in a particular mix of femininity and authority with Thatcher:

Margaret Thatcher, that's what she did – a woman can have a very satisfying sexual relationship with one of her entourage without it ever coming to anything. If you are a woman in charge, you've got a retinue of young men whose duty it is to provide your every need. You're a bit like the Queen. You never carry your own money. You never buy your own ticket. (Barbara Castle cited in McDougall 1998: 53)

She flirted outrageously with some of the men. I am sure if you looked at her behaviour in the lobby when some of the men who were part of her inner circle, the Tebbits and Parkinson's were with her, her manner and her body language were quite different. (Teresa Gorman cited in McDougall 1998: 53)

Instead of counterposing male behaviour with feminine dress, whereby women have to be either masculine or feminine, it is possible to see how they are related. After all, Thatcher held the two together in her particular configuration of masculinity and femininity and positions of authority in the body politic. Because the role of an MP has become sedimented into a male embodiment, when women enact the same competences and attributes they are accused of denying their femininity. They are seen to be acting as men but not as women and accused of mimicking the men. However, given that there had never been a female prime minister, it is hard to see how a woman could avoid mimicking the men who have occupied the role. Indeed, it is precisely because politicians are imagined as men that, when women try to behave like men, they are viewed with suspicion. Coupled with this, femininity is defined as a lack of masculine qualities. As pointed out by Alvesson and Due Billing, an established community of men can find it hard to 'read' the talk, appearance and actions of women in senior positions; consequently women will represent a 'source of uncertainty' and 'be inclined to face unease, scepticism and even resistance and hostility.' (1997: 109). Suspected of lacking the relevant competences, women have to be exceptional politicians in order to get on. They have to shine. Because people do not expect the relevant competences to be embodied in a female body, women have to 'over do' their performance of these competences to make up for the suspected lack. Not wanting to be seen as lacking, Thatcher masqueraded the so-called male competences in an even more exaggerated fashion than men did.

Furthermore, an exaggerated form of male behaviour required an exaggeratedly feminine style of dress. Because Thatcher's behaviour was 'masculine', which is constituted through the exclusion of the feminine, she had to avoid being seen as lacking in femininity. Margaret Thatcher was caught between contradictory ideals of being like a politician (defined in masculine terms) and being feminine; thus she had to manage the risk of being negatively evaluated for being either unpolitician like or unfeminine. Thus we have the phenomena of highly feminine suits, jewellery and general attire. It is important to note that a male style of behaviour combined with an exaggeratedly feminine style of dress could be accepted in a place where masculine and feminine binaries are firmly entrenched. However, a female body displaying masculine behaviour in less feminine or androgynous dress would have been considered indecorous. In other words, a 'suited and booted' middle-class female body in the body politic would undoubtedly have been seen as grotesque and improper (Arthurs and Grimshaw 1999).

Her voice was specifically trained to not be too feminine in pitch, because it was assumed that the deeper and lower tone could be a source of strength rather than irritation. Perhaps Thatcher represented an acceptable fusion of femininity and masculinity within the confines of existing gender directives – hence the maxim, 'Dress like a lady and act like a man'. After all, as pointed out by Butler, deviations from the acceptable attire of femininity attract penalties. When women are dependent upon the support of other (largely male) MPs, this is perhaps a risk they cannot afford to take. Moving outside authorised boundaries of what is 'viable' behaviour is a risky business.

What we must not forget in our in-depth engagements with gender analysis is how 'race' is also a part of the script politicians enact. Too often, race only figures when 'black' women are studied; it is also a part of white political femininities, even though it is often disavowed. Thatcher's toughness was entwined with empire, war and foreign policy. Hence 'race' and nation and not just gender were an implicit part of the white femininity she animated in her speech and body. In an in-depth study, *Thatcher, Politics and Fantasy*, Heather Nunn notes:

> Thatcher's image of national leadership – surrounded by the latest technology of the battlefield – conjured up fantasies of imperial venture and heroic narratives of masculine courage and strength in the face of adversity, of defending one's own land alongside the righteous incursion of another's territory. Her speeches throughout the 1980s were replete with references to 'our' victory in World War Two, as were her numerous invocations of the wartime Prime Minister Winston Churchill, who was a model of masterful leadership that she sought to adopt. (2002: 10)

While Churchill saw women MPs as an invasion, here was a woman who trail-blazed a heroic self with reverence for Britain's victorious wartime leader. In addition, she hailed allegorical female symbols of the national, most especially Britannia. Her particular fusion galvanised powerful historical female symbols of women as fighters, protectors and brave defenders of the nation's spirit. Commenting on Thatcher's fusion, Marina Warner mentions that she combined 'Britannia's resoluteness, Boadicea's courage with a proper housewifely demeanour' (1996: 53). Their courage was combined with masculine adventure, military might and entrepreneurial renewal. Her tough, fighting talk is softened by her appearance and made familial with reference to the home, while at the same time being the righteous protector of the national hearth. Military might and defence, the most protected of male domains, are grafted on to the whole notion of taking care of a nation under threat. Military tanks and nuclear weapons were all a part of her political arsenal. These were, in her fusion, articulated with acceptable and attractive versions of femininity. Thus we have the silk headscarves, pearls, handbags and fitted suits.

Doing Gender/MP Scripts Differently

Many of the women MPs thought that Margaret Thatcher's way was only one way of 'doing' gender/MP and that there are other ways of being a woman in Parliament. Mo Mowlam was often mentioned as an alternative, positive role model. Interestingly, some journalists scorned the praise that has been granted to Mo Mowlam for handling the Northern Ireland peace process in a 'different' manner from the set mould, by attributing to Mowlam an affective, emotional style of leadership that was lacking in clear rational thinking. This description, of course, repeats the old mantra where reason (masculinity) and affectivity (femininity) are separated in an asymmetrical gendered dichotomy. Given that women are in a rather tenuous situation as 'space invaders' in the first place, the expectation that their mere presence as individuals will be enough to shift the political style of the place is unrealistic. Much more is required if we are to reverse the institutionally embedded masculine advantage. It entails a huge overhaul of the political imagination, especially the unspoken representation of the male body as the 'universal' body.

The Imperial/Legitimate Language

Becoming Human: the Civility of Language

Fanon provides some vivid scenes of the play between personhood, language, civility and 'race':

> In the election campaign of 1945, Aimé Césaire, who was seeking a deputy's seat, addressed a large audience in the boy's school in Fort-de-France. In the middle of his speech a woman fainted. The next day, an acquaintance told me about this, and commented: *Français a té tellement chaud que l'a femme la tombé malcadi*. The power of language! (Fanon 1986: 39).

André Breton said of Césaire, 'Here is a black man who handles the French language as no white man today can.' Commenting on this remark Fanon states:

> even though Breton may be stating a fact, I do not see why there should be a paradox, anything to underline, for in truth M. Aimé Césaire is a native of Martinique and a university graduate (1986: 40).

Breton clearly has an enormous admiration in witnessing Césaire conversing in what is considered to be perfect French, which is for Breton all the more beautiful because it is articulated by a black man of the French colony of Martinique. The surprise and pleasure of witnessing a 'black' uttering perfect French was clearly a combination that was a little too much to bear for the woman, causing her to faint at what for her was an astonishing sight. Fanon highlights these examples in order to consider the categorisations that lie behind the incongruity of the 'black' body articulating the French language. He begs us to think about why exactly this sight is shocking. Why is the combination such a pleasurable surprise?

For Fanon, these 'looks', however compassionate they may be, point to the power of the imperial language. Speaking French is a property that endows the colonised with civility and honour. There is a metamorphic transformative property attached to a 'black' body who speaks the coloniser's language. Noting the transformation he states: 'The Negro of the Antilles will be proportionately whiter – that is, he will come closer to being a real human being – in direct ratio to his mastery of the French language' (1986: 18).

Even in enlightened circles, and Breton was indeed committed to anti-racism, the respect for perfect French is so entrenched, however unconscious this may be, that, when it is articulated by the denigrated, it becomes an enticing mixture. Such is the social magic (cf. Taussig 1997) of the imperial language. By competently speaking the legitimate imperial language, 'The colonized is elevated above his jungle status in proportion to his adoption of the mother country's cultural standards. He becomes whiter as he renounces his blackness, his jungle' (Fanon 1986: 18). Performance of this 'higher' form of language enables colonials to 'enjoy a certain position of honour' (1986: 19). Competency in the imperial language is a sign of a black person's ability to rise to some of the heights of white civilisation, leading white people to admiringly remark, 'He talks like a book' (1986: 21). Thus 'the Negro is appraised in terms of the extent of his assimilation' to the imperial ways of being (1986: 36). Reflecting on the role of language upon his own location Fanon notes:

> Rather more than a year ago in Lyon, I remember, in a lecture I had drawn a parallel between Negro and European poetry, and a French acquaintance told me enthusiastically, "At bottom you are a white man." The fact that I had been able to investigate so interesting a problem through the white man's language gave me honorary citizenship (1986: 38).

In the chapter 'The Negro and Language', Fanon offers a compelling and critical observation of the fact that French associated with the 'culture of the mother country' carries the symbolic power of being 'the language of the civilizing nation'[1] (1986: 18). Whilst he focuses on the specific role of French in the Antilles, his analysis, as he himself says, can be applied to other colonial and postcolonial contexts. Language is one of a range of methods that have been utilised to induce rationality, civility and civilisation in foreign bodies: 'To speak a language is to take on a world, a culture. The Antilles Negro who wants to be white will be the whiter as he gains greater mastery of the cultural tool that language is' (Fanon 1986: 38).

Language is intimately connected to governmentality. The association of European languages with rational thinking, the values of civilisation and intelligence is part and parcel of the long routes of colonisation that make our postcolonial times today. The stamp of superiority and assimilation has been, and continues to be, borne by language in the workings of 'racial governmentality' (Hesse 1997). Questions of national and international governance have informed the practical work of measurement in everyday encounters on the street as well as within institutions. Paraphrasing Fanon, Goldberg states:

> language assists in the domestication of the native or racialized people and culture, imposing the order of the Logos upon the presumed flux of a people supposedly lacking rationality and the *Geist* of world history ... The Logos borne by European language is supposed to drag primitive society into the modern, the rational, the historical (1997: 97–8).

Today different languages and accents from around the globe slide past and into each other on the streets of Western métropoles. However, in the higher echelons of social life, in professional occupations, it is not only the imperial language that is a requirement but rather a specifically classed form of speaking: what Breton termed 'perfect French' or what Bourdieu has incisively coined as the 'legitimate language'. Language is intrinsic to the somatic norm in the professions, and the imperial/ legitimate language is a key tacit requirement.

Eliciting Tacit Requirements: the 'Soft Things'

Processes of inclusion and exclusion are often extremely subtle, and involve informal rules of behaviour that are rarely explicitly discussed or mentioned. In all social worlds, including the world of occupations and professions, there are 'tacit requirements', which can operate as 'real principles of selection or exclusion without ever being formally stated' (Bourdieu 1984: 102).[2]

While conducting in-depth interviews with Black and Asian professionals, instead of holding the conversation with the usual victim-focused reductive line of questioning that seeks information on marginalisation and barriers, I asked the question: 'What has enabled you to rise within your occupational hierarchy?' Having an acute awareness of the infinitesimal ways in which people are measured in the professions, a world based on distinctions, a 'black' civil servant to whom I put the question 'What is important to career success and how people rise in the ranks of the senior civil service?' observed that you need to possess the right 'soft things':

Soft things meaning how you might behave in a group ... how you dress, how you speak, how you interact are probably more important than some people realise here and if you appreciate that and take appropriate measures then that's more likely to help you. But in the end you've got to have the basic good work and then you've got to have the other things to help you.

The location of specific social codes (the 'soft things') as being important to success resonates with Bourdieu's theory that certain attributes or habituses – defined as 'internalized embodied schemes' acquired 'in the course of individual history' (1984: 467) – operate as symbolic, cultural, social and economic capital. These qualify people to rise in particular occupations and professions. This particular senior civil servant was acutely aware of the rules of existence in the dynamics of his specific institutional context. Commenting on his own social construction, he mentioned that he had acquired these 'soft' ways by observing and listening to other senior members in the institution. He spoke of how he had managed to 'pick up' the appropriate behaviour. He was conscious of the fact that 'the way you put things' seemed to be important. He stressed that the 'manner of speech' must be 'polite but firm'. And he noted that it is necessary to 'defend your corner but not to oversell' the point being made. Interestingly, he had consciously identified these informal rules of behaviour, so that he could perform in a manner considered appropriate to becoming a trusted and respected colleague. In his case, he had acquired what Bourdieu refers to as 'practical knowledge' of the normative codes in the higher echelons of this institution by quite deliberately acculturating the legitimate infinitesimal codes of behaviour.

Other 'successful' employees may not be so conscious of the assimilative pressure posed by the normative culture of their occupations. Indeed, they may have acquired the 'soft things' spontaneously by moving through 'civilising' upper/middle-class spaces. Hence they do not need to be so contrived in the acquisition and articulation of these skills, as they prevail automatically. The world (described by Bourdieu as objective structures and social fields) lives in our habitus (incorporated structures), not as a simple imprint that determines us, but rather as something we activate through our practices, however unconscious and automatic this social action may be (1998: viii). The schemas of the habitus operate 'beyond the reach of introspective scrutiny or control by the will', as they become embedded 'in the most automatic gestures or the apparently most insignificant techniques of the body-ways of walking or blowing one's nose, ways of eating or talking' (1984: 466).

We are more likely to become aware of the ways in which the dispositions are acquired when there is discordance between what one's habitus is and what one is required to be – when, for instance, there is a 'mismatch between the scholastic mode of acquisition and "high society" situations.' (Bourdieu 1984: 571, n. 11). Bourdieu refers to this as the Don Quixote effect. In the specific case of the civil servant (as discussed above) he had become conscious of subtle indices of manner or bearing which were 'analogous' to the higher civil service. His positionality was in some respects one of discordance, a position that enabled him to *see* and *name* what may be invisible to those who are automatically the norm.

I want to underline that these subtle codes are signs which are central to the discriminatory practices through which social spaces are formed; they are not secondary. The desired social skills for mixing, meeting strangers and the appropriate etiquette are as stated by Lemert 'the measuring lines whereby the structuring power of prestige, authority and income come down upon practical people'. And a 'closer look at race, gender, and class allows at least a first glimpse at the nefarious manners by which the dominant enforce their codes of social differences' (Lemert 1997: 168–9). Language is central to these processes.

Language and Symbolic Power

The ability to articulate the 'legitimate' language is one of the central, if not the central, 'soft things' essential to coexistence in the professions. Command, authority and respect are more readily conferred on those who communicate in what Bourdieu refers to as the 'legitimate language'. People are much more likely to be heard if they speak in the 'legitimate' tones, syntax and grammar because this is the hegemonic language, the voice of reason. Noting the variability of each form of capital in different fields, he stresses that each profession has particular attributes that count as capital. Language, however, is one attribute that is especially important in marking 'distinction' across all formal social spaces.

The acquisition of the 'national language' is absolutely key to the performance of public positions. Thus language can be viewed as a central element of the corporeality of authority. The 'state language' is 'obligatory on official occasions and in official places (schools, public administrations, political institutions, etc.), this state language becomes the theoretical norm against which all linguistic practices are objectively measured' (Bourdieu 1992: 45). Bearing symbolic power, the national language is considered to be the only way of speaking, whilst other ways of speaking (slang/regional) are viewed as inferior vulgarities. Language acts as an extremely important marker of distinction: 'the competence necessary in order to speak the legitimate language which, depending on social inheritance, re-translates social distinctions into the specifically symbolic logic of differential deviations, or in short, distinction (Bourdieu 1992: 55).

This legitimate language is the preserve of the upper classes. Those who do not have this class exposure through family can acquire it within the educational system. After all, it is the language that is endorsed by schools and universities, particularly élite educational institutions. 'Grammarians' and those who suffer from 'hypercorrection' diligently police the scene and obscene the 'correct' written and spoken language.

On the specific question of language and social measurement, in relation to 'race', Bourdieu gave some thought to communication between 'settlers' and 'natives' in colonial and postcolonial contexts. He stressed that any analysis of linguistic encounters must consider the power dynamics. He states: 'if a French person talks with an Algerian, or a black American to a WASP, it is not two persons who speak to each other but, through them, the colonial history in its entirety, or the whole history of the economic, political and cultural subjugation of blacks' (1992: 144).

On the specific question of language as an assimilative device he remarks: 'every linguistic interaction between whites and blacks is constrained by the encompassing structural relation between their respective appropriations of English, and by the power imbalance, which sustains it and gives the arbitrary imposition of middle-class, "white" English its air of naturalness' (1992: 143). Despite the centrality of colonialism and race to the formation of Bourdieu's thought,[3] the level of detail he brought to the analysis of legitimate language in terms of class was not sustained in regard to race. Hence the need for Fanon.[4]

Acceptable/Respectable Bodies

In institutions the imperial legitimate language clearly carries weight. It enables racialised bodies to become 'honourable' 'civilised' humans. Moreover, it has a huge significance for who gets accepted in respectable positions. Competency in the white, upper/middle-class (state) language, what Fanon refers to as the 'white man's language', is absolutely critical to the inclusion of black bodies in the white 'civilised' spaces of the professions. When established institutions open their doors to postcolonial bodies, they have a strong preference for those who have assimilated the 'mother country's' legitimate language. Proficiency in the legitimate national language plays a decisive role in the selection of black bodies for professional spaces. They bear the signs of cultural refinement.[5] As an instrument of the governance of 'civility', the acquisition of the imperial/legitimate language is able to take racialised bodies through a passage of rites to becoming honourable human beings.

The importance of specific educational spaces (such as public schools and Oxbridge) for inscribing a body with what is referred to as the 'correct' use of the English language cannot be underestimated. Indeed, those black senior civil servants who had been to public schools in England or to Oxbridge noted that these experiences had helped them to feel comfortable in the senior civil service. It was mentioned that the language they had acquired in these educational establishments was 'the language of the civil service'. It is an advantage to have gone to Oxbridge because:

> the way you write is very Oxbridge type. Being able to write well matters a lot. The standard of your analysis may not matter so much but the actual veneer of how you write matters a lot.

Thus the inscription of competence in the legitimate (classed and racialised) language through élite educational institutions becomes transferable to the professions. If for a moment we think back to the argument made by Mills, that all spaces are racialised, and that 'The Racial Contract norms (and races) space, demarcating civil and wild spaces' (1997: 41), then we can see how Oxbridge, as a white space which is associated with refinement, can 'civilise' otherwise wild bodies. Along with public schools, Oxbridge is considered to be one of the most 'civilised' educational institutions in the world. Thus the experience of black bodies in this space is not insignificant. Their journey through these spaces has a 'civilising' effect on those 'naturally' associated with 'other' spaces. These institutions make racialised bodies much more amenable to 'refined' company. Pleasant-speaking hybrid postcolonial black bodies, who 'speak like a book', are much more suited to white élite spaces. They are, after all, the acceptable respectable faces of black bodies.[6] Thus far, I have been discussing the importance of 'civilising' processes to the inclusion of racialised minorities in the senior civil service. Similar dynamics occur in other institutions.

Those who don the right way of speaking and the associated manners as a white mask on their non-white skins do not simply pick it up and put it down as and when required. This would be too much of a mechanical and voluntaristic reading of the mask. Instead, we need to think of it as being acquired slowly through time by moving through white 'civilising' spaces (educational, neighbourhoods, friends and institutional positions). Existence within and movement through these spaces facilitates the acquisition of the necessary competences for a successful, often unconscious, performance of what Fanon (1986) has termed 'mimicry'.

In the next section, I want to consider the performative menace posed by the donning of the white mask, through mimicry, and the complex position of being unassimilable.

Performative

Feminists have been particularly keen to emphasise the subversive force of the repetition of masculine performances by women. Repeated with a difference, the normative is at once disrupted and denaturalised (for a summary of the performative see Bell 1999). The work of Riviere (1986), Irigaray and Butler has been especially influential for a consideration of the menace posed by women in male outfits. Chapter 5 utilised Butler to elucidate the re-enactment of occupational scripts by women within the confines of existing gendered directives. Her analysis enables a consideration of the sedimented context within which gendered bodies are orchestrated, as well as of the possibilities of a different sort of repeating. For 'race' and especially when it is anchored to class, the analysis of these feminists is much more limited.[7] In an indirect reference to 'race', during the course of a critique of Bourdieu, which has now become the site of considerable debate within feminism (Lovell 2002; McNay 2002), Butler seems to be a little too quick to stress the subversive.

The performative in Bourdieu, most specifically in relation to the speech act, is critiqued by Butler. She says he overemphasises the constraints posed by social context in a way that leaves little room for transformation and 'inadvertently forecloses the possibility of an agency that emerges from the margins of power' (1999: 156).[8] Butler wants to emphasise how dominant discourses can be subverted for radical ends by those who do not occupy official positions of power. So, for instance, 'black' leaders can harness the accepted language of equality to radical ends even while they do so in the legitimate idioms (for a discussion of Rosa Parks see Butler 1997a).

Keen to spot the transformative, Butler is unable however to question why the articulation has to occur through legitimate idioms for the demands to be heard in the first place. If we go back to Fanon's discussion of Césaire, Butler's blind spot becomes even more obvious. Césaire was clearly articulating a radical black agenda, in élite idioms (Gibson 2003). He was a black anti-colonial revolutionary. However, what Fanon draws our attention to is the power of the imperial language. The metamorphic quality of this idiom transforms an invisible or even denigrated body into one that is entitled to be heard. And we know from Breton's comments that Césaire was respected for uttering a form of French that was, in Bourdieu's sense, the legitimate French. Butler fails to adequately consider the force of the racialised and classed directives that confine who speaks or, rather, who and what type of speech is *heard* in the public realm. We know that the mismatch between habitus and the social field of official speech means that those who don't come from privileged class backgrounds or have not undergone élite educational training do not automatically have the advantaged habitus.

The 'Menace' of Presence?

In his discussion of an anglicised Indian educated in English who works in the Indian civil service during the period of British colonial rule, Homi Bhabha (1994) argues that this figure represents an interpellation of colonial subjects according to metropolitan norms. He states that the colonial subjects who mimic Englishmen become the subject of a difference that is 'almost the same, but not quite' (1994: 89). These persons can behave like their masters – but they cannot become exact copies, as they are not quite white or European. They produce a partial representation of the metropolitan culture, but in doing so they underline their own difference from it. It is in this point of difference that Bhabha locates a 'menace' in their mimicry. He argues that, even though they mimic metropolitan norms, they are not simply copying because the process of becoming the same is much more dynamic. Bhabha insists that mimicry is not merely submissive to the colonial power, but that 'mimicry is at once resemblance and 'menace' (1994: 86).

Mimicry is a menace because it is an inappropriate representation of the metropolitan culture – it is the right words coming out of the wrong mouths. Bhabha says 'mimic man' (and we might add mimic woman[9]) is disruptive because s/he shows that the 'identity' of the coloniser is not a matter of essence, as implied by the equation between white skin and civilisation, but rather is itself a discursive construct that sustains power relations. The assumption that 'white' is essentially superior to 'black'

– the premise of European self-consciousness and the justification of its colonial activities – is called into question by this colonial encounter. The qualities that have historically been constituted to be essentially white create disorientation, a disorder and a menace when they are displayed by non-white bodies. When the features of the Englishman are reflected back to him via the body of the Indian, this is a moment of self-assurance for him. But it is also a moment of displacement, as he is shifted out of his exclusive subject position by what is quite a different image of himself. This slightly tilted transposition thus carries menacing effects that unwittingly distress the coloniser.

Whether we can see the semblance of racialised professionals to their white counterparts as a menace, in Bhabha's sense, is nevertheless open to question. Their presence in these white places certainly does disturb the sedimented centuries-old natural order of this institution. They disrupt the naturalised relationship between authority, seniority and the associated competences with white bodies. Unlike Bhabha however, I want to emphasise that their presence is not a menace to the extent that it leaves the normative power of whiteness intact. The surveillance of governmentality in Bhabha gets played down because of the due emphasis he wants to place on processes of ambivalence.[10] Or, as Chow asks of Bhabha's mimic man: 'it is the ambivalences, the contradictions, and the fissures, always already inherent to the dominant modes of articulation, that open things up, so to speak. What is the genuine import of such openings? Whom do they benefit?' (2002: 106).

The disruption that is caused by mimicry is not sufficient to challenge the power of whiteness to define itself and the subsequent culture in the civil service as the, undeclared, standard. The placement of specific normative ways of being as central and others as marginal is hardly disturbed. It also does not problematise the placement of these very specific central norms, standards and procedures as universal and as racially unmarked. In fact, much of the power of these standards derives from the liberal construction of them as disembodied. Hence, mimicry of these norms by black civil servants does not threaten the assimilative pressures on those who want to succeed at senior levels in the civil service to 'become white or disappear' (Fanon cited in Goldberg 1996: 185).

Elaborating on the notion of self-erasure, Goldberg highlights the fact that:

> black people are faced with the dilemma that the principal mode of progress and self-elevation open to them is precisely through self-denial, through the effacement, the obliteration, of their blackness. They are predicated, that is,

upon the possibility of rendering a significant feature of their self-definition invisible, if not altogether effaced. This invisibility, in turn, is effected through the necessity of recognition by whites which is begrudgingly extended only at the cost of the invisibility of blackness. (1996: 185)

There is very little room for the coexistence of difference in the senior civil service, except of the kind discussed by Bhabha in relation to mimicry. Different bodies can exist in the senior civil service so long as they mimic. It is important to recognise that this is what the acceptance of cultural diversity amounts to in most organisations in Britain. It means that they allow for the existence of 'different' phenotypical bodies amongst their ranks, so long as they mimic the norm, whilst the norm itself is not problematised. Although Bhabha chooses to stress the dynamic and productive side of mimicry, like Fanon and Goldberg, Bhabha does, however, offer some acknowledgement of the denial and erasure involved in this process. He notes that 'mimicry emerges as the representation of a difference that is itself a process of disavowal' (1994: 86).

Whilst black civil servants can recognise that they are like a 'white master'[11] and need to be so that they can succeed, they also have a highly developed sense of their difference. They are not just conscious of their difference but also aware that this difference is not marked as some multicultural, pluralist recognition of difference. Rather, it is marked as a negative difference *per se*. To reiterate a point made at the beginning of this chapter, it is a negative difference that is located in relation to 'ordinary', 'natural', unraced and unracialised whiteness, what Hazel Carby has called 'the (white) point in space from which we tend to identify difference' (1992: 193).

In embodying the right words in the wrong mouths these 'black' bodies in white spaces do represent a menace. But at the same time we need to bear in mind that the sheer novelty of their presence in these institutional domains means that they exist under the constant spotlight of surveillance. In this respect they are suspiciously matter out of place. In a situation where racial difference is viewed negatively, it really is an honour if one's racial difference is not noticed and one is treated the same, allowing black artists, writers, lecturers or civil servants to just become generic practitioners where their colour and ethnicity are of no significance. The desire to become the same is itself indicative of the power of the liberal myth of 'colour-blindness' and the consequent centrifugal force of the somatic norm. The so-called 'colour-blind' standards and norms of the professions ultimately impose whiteness as the norm, as a specific set of norms and experiences are written into the standards.

–7–

Becoming Insiders

It is commonplace to speak of women or racialised minorities as being marginal outsiders to organisations. There is however a reluctance to face up to the extent to which they are insiders, partly because what is made visible – in terms of comportment, manner and networks – makes it difficult to wave the mantle of marginality in simplistic terms. It is necessary to be an insider to some degree to even be allowed in, to exist. And you have to be even more of an insider to rise through the hierarchies of institutions. Having stepped through the threshold to the inside of an occupation, all staff, to varying degrees, partake in the chequer-board terrain within which careers are made. This is a playing-field that is riddled with networks, conflicts, struggles, cliques, judgements, infinitesimal sources of measurement and social cloning from the top to the bottom.

In the last chapter we saw how a certain bodily hexis and most specifically the ability to speak the imperial–legitimate language is central to the unspoken tacit requirements of senior posts, even though these regularities are not explicitly codified. This chapter continues to complicate the inside/outside position of 'space invaders' by taking a further look at how they are in significant respects included. They have investments in their positions and participate in a quagmire of social relations of endorsement. The notion of ontological complicity helps us to elucidate the differentiated levels of inclusion that pertain in the space of institutions.[1] Ontological denial of 'race', gender and class is part of being an insider. It is embedded in institutional narratives. Thus the latter part of the chapter will discuss the contortions that result in naming embodiment. Altogether it will address the contradictory and tenuous position of 'space invaders' generated from different degrees of ontological complicity/denial.

Investment in the Game

Even though occupational fields comprise shifting constellations of power and conflict, all professionals have a degree of investment in their field. Their positions may not be centrally located; none the less, as practitioners, they are on the inside by way of participating in the game.

> We have an *investment in the game*, *illusio* (from *ludus*, the game): players are taken in by the game, they oppose one another, sometimes with ferocity, only to the extent that they concur in their belief (*doxa*) in the game and the stakes; they grant these a recognition that escapes questioning. Players agree, by the mere fact of playing and not by way of a 'contract,' that the game is worth playing, that it is 'worth the candle,' and this collusion is the very basis of their competition. (Bourdieu 1992: 98)

The investment in the game is the first and most simple sense in which women and racialised minorities are, however differentially placed and committed, on the inside. The word 'game' should not lead us to assume that people are conscious strategists or that there is an overall conductor/ instructor to this game. Careful to steer clear of rational action theory, Bourdieu states that a person is not 'like a gambler organizing his stakes on the basis of perfect information about his chances of winning' (1995: 54). Processes of participation and inclusion are much more subtle.

The notion that competition is primarily based on merit is intrinsic to the narrative of the professions; in a most obvious sense, it's assumed that members have professed the 'objective' requirements of their fields. One of the abiding attractions of meritocracy is the prospect of being measured on the basis of ability and skill instead of ilk and patronage. The merit principle represents openness – via assessment – which is undoubtedly a liberation from the closed coteries of patronage. Professionalisation has not, however, meant that recruitment and promotion are based purely on measures derived from instruments (exams and appraisals) that are cold, clean and devoid of the messiness of culture and power. Personal patronage has, rather, transmuted from closed fraternities to complex assemblages of professional patronage – borne in the scholastic and bureaucratic terms of peer reviews, references and performance indicators. The social organisation of recruitment and promotion is made through circles, competing and overlapping, of mutual admiration, all of which are absolutely vital to how careers are made. Whoever one is, the endorsement and support of significant others, whichever field one is employed in, are pivotal to getting on.

To be in a career, you have already been part and parcel of the practice of endorsement, even though you may not be conscious of it. The higher you rise, the more you are party to the mechanisms of affirmation. As there is a continuous and dynamic struggle over power within and between fields, the endorsements need not necessarily come in a straight line from those actors who are centrally located. They may also come via newly emerging and competing factions. All employees concur in this chequer-board terrain, although the degree to which they concur varies.

Sponsors and Advocates: Gaining Weight

Advocates (or, as they are popularly known in management-speak, mentors) operate in every field. They are, as Bourdieu says, a person's 'most powerful protectors' (2001: 91). In order to rise in hierarchies, everyone needs advocates to vouch for the fact that they are a trusted and respected pair of hands. Those who don't fit the traditional somatic norm in the higher echelons of the public realm, that is, women and racialised minorities, most especially need advocates. In order to get on, all bodies need advocates and exposure to key players in the field; however, the 'newcomers', depending on the degree of their 'strangeness', desperately require the seal of approval. Marshall (1984) says that women are 'travellers' in a male world who need the assistance of mentors to succeed.[2] In some senses we could say that women are able to enter male spaces when established insiders welcome them, support them, in some ways adopt them and show them the way in this somewhat new and 'alien' territory. Thus a sponsor can facilitate this boundary crossing.[3] The further away they are from the somatic norm, the more they are in need of the blessing which facilitates a specific rite of passage, and, the more centrally located their advocates are to the field in question, the more reassurance is borne in their word. Thus the carriage of the supporter has an impact upon one's own standing.

Visibility is crucial to all the professions; it is necessary for one to be known amongst one's peers for opportunities to be opened up. Visibility comes from jumping through the right hoops that offer opportunities for exposure and respect from influential quarters. Specific activities that take a person outside the strict duties of their in-tray can give social exposure to key players in the field. These openings can be especially facilitated by advocates, sponsors or mentors. In addition, certain appointments, because of their proximity to influential players in specific departments or institutions, provide the opportunity to be known and trusted amongst those who carry weight. Through exposure to significant agents, there is a possibility that those people, who will themselves be located in competing circles, will become personal advocates. Being respected operators in the field, the recommendations of advocates, through either informal or formal means, such as references, supervisory assessments and appraisals, carry weight. Their recognition functions as a warranty and a stamp of approval from the right quarters. As social capital is a 'durable network of more or less institutionalized relationships of mutual acquaintance and recognition' (Bourdieu and Wacquant 2002: 119), they are trusted to give their word on the capabilities of a particular person because their own reputation is bound up with these relationships. Clearly, if the colleague or pupil does not deliver, they risk losing some of their own weight in the field.

Peer review and the need for advocacy do not only operate at the grand points of a person's career – in other words, when applying for appointments. They also operate on a daily basis in formal, informal and coincidental gatherings. Numerous recommendations are made without an explicit process of advertisement, application and competition. Selection runs through the workings of organisational channels as a matter of routine. So, for instance, curators select artists on the basis of visibility and recommendations. Special governmental committees and advisory groups are formed by seeking (sniffing) out who is 'reputable'. Academics are invited to submit chapters to books or to journals through mutual networks. Invitations to speak and to join research projects are conducted through informal means of selection. Thus people are included and excluded through silent and invisible manoeuvres as standard course of play. These small choices can be key for building profiles and making selections for significant projects and appointments.

Social Cloning

One of the major anxieties of handing over an opportunity to a new person is the concern: can this person be trusted with the job? Is she or he a safe pair of hands? Being a known entity and a 'safe pair of hands' is elemental to the decision. The tendency to grant trust to 'known' entities provides ripe conditions for encouraging social cloning, identikit or approximate, in terms of either social background, habitus or ideas.

Those who fit in with the existing somatic norm, however disputed this terrain may be, due to internal and external battles to define the boundaries of disciplines and fields, are supported in the quagmire of webs that embody social movement. Support for others who have an affinity to oneself is at the same time an act of self-affirmation and self-reproduction. The 'fit' of the person is especially important for promotability to top positions. Herein is contained the tendency for social cloning and social reproduction. In the senior civil service, for instance, when seniors look 'for a successor to themselves, they tend to look for somebody who will have the same style' (interviewee). Looking for themselves in their prodigies, these seniors reproduce certain social types at the top of organisations.

Social cloning not only occurs at the level of somatics, ways of carrying the body, gestures and mannerisms, as well as a likeness in social background and social networks. It is also manifested in ideas, opinions, political perspective and social taste in general. Anyone too different and radical can very easily be labelled as a maverick or someone who is out of bounds for support and endorsement. They can become subject to a form of blocking that is not explicit, overtly conscious or conspiratorial in any way, but is none the less critical to the direction of their career.

The combined nexus of social cloning and professional patronage can stall careers. Looking at a particular discipline in academia, David Sibley (1997) has analysed how Du Bois's contribution to urban geography was sidelined by a key player in the field. He argues that Robert Parks's powerful position in the making of urban geography and sociology at the University of Chicago enabled him to define the methodological and political terms of research on the black population and race relations. Du Bois's study of race and the city, most famously published as *The Philadelphia Negro*, was not granted the endorsement and patronage given by Park to other 'black' academics. This was due to both political and methodological reasons. His methodology was too much in the interpretative and hermeneutic tradition for a Chicago School that was desperate to establish itself as a serious discipline by mimicking the natural sciences. In addition, Du Bois's politics on race conflicted with the assimilationist and apolitical slant preferred by Burgess and Park, 'who had the power to marginalize or block alternative perspectives.' (Sibley 1997: 154). Sibley mentions that 'Park disapproved of the politicization of race because political commitment was incompatible with a scientific approach to understanding' (1997: 150). He goes as far as stating that Black academics 'had to conform to Park's view of urban society if they were to make any impact, and DuBois's perspective certainly differed in fundamental respects from Park's' (1997: 151).

Clearly there is a struggle over the terms that should define any field, academic or otherwise:

one person's pedigree can become another's mark of infamy, one's coat of arms another's insult, and vice versa, are there to remind us that the university field is, like any field, the locus of a struggle to determine the conditions and the criteria of legitimate membership and legitimate hierarchy, that is, to determine which properties are pertinent, effective and liable to function as capital. (Bourdieu 2001: 11)

When we think about how 'race' impacts upon actual institutions we are led to consider the importance of 'likeness'. That is social cloning in terms of social connections, theoretical persuasions and politics, as well as comportment and manner. Those who engage in the 'legitimate' idioms of various disciplines are more likely to be welcomed into the domain. As we witness a number of policy initiatives under the banner of 'diversity', the 'guarded' tolerance in the desire for difference carries in the unspoken small print of assimilation a 'drive for sameness'. Through these processes the kind of questions that are asked as well as the voices that are amenable to being heard within the regular channels of the art world, academia or other fields of work, can become seriously stunted. Multiculturalism, internationalism and cosmopolitanism have their own administrative logic for regulating and managing 'cultural difference' (Maharaj 1999: 6–7).

As an artist, Eddie Chambers asks, 'how much accommodation do we have to make ... to suit "other" palates, "other" tastes'. He argues, 'the art establishment is looking for people it can embrace as "one of us", people who can "speak our language"' (1999: 26–31).

What gets defined as 'wild' or out of bounds is, of course, subject to the elasticity of occupational boundaries. It also depends on how the 'wildness' is strategically disguised in the general 'feel for the game' (discussed below) and whether it is supported by influential advocates who carry weight (as discussed above).

A Feel For the Game

It is important to underline that 'co-optation techniques always aim to select "the man", the whole person, the *habitus*' (Bourdieu 2001: 57). People are sifted out or endorsed on the basis of a 'corporeal hexis, of a style of expression and thought, and of all those "indefinable somethings", pre-eminently physical, which we call "spirit"' (Bourdieu 2001: 56). Implicit in getting on is what Bourdieu calls a feel for the game (*le sens de jeu*) or a practical sense (*le sens pratique*). You have to have this sense to be appointed and promoted. At the same time, though, people are differentiated in the extent to which they are included and the extent to which they are insiders in accordance with how well their habitus is adjusted to the demands of the field.

Practice is not, however, simply the result of 'conscious and deliberate intentions of the authors' and neither is it a 'mechanical reaction' (Bourdieu 1977: 73). Concerned to sidestep the extremes of the two binaries determinism and voluntarism, structures and individuals or objectivism and subjectivism, Bourdieu deliberately uses the word strategies over the common language of social rules, which he says placed researchers in the position of 'God the father watching the social actors like puppets controlled by the strings of structure'. At the same, time he is keen to strip the word strategy of its 'naively teleological connotations' (1990b: 10). He states, 'practical sense or, if you prefer, what sports players call a feel for the game – a practical mastery acquired by experience of the game' is 'one which works outside conscious control and discourse (in the way that, for instance, techniques of the body do)' (1990b: 61).

Social practice is thus not rational. Instead, it is part of a process of improvisation, which in turn is structured by cultural orientations, personal trajectories and the ability to play the game of social interaction. This is explained further by an example from sport:

> Action guided by a 'feel for the game' has all the appearances of the rational action that an impartial observer, endowed with all the necessary information and capable of mastering it rationally, would deduce. And yet it is not based on reason. You need only think of the impulsive decision made by the tennis player who runs up to the net, to understand that it has nothing in common with the learned construction that the coach, after analysis, draws up in order to explain it and deduce communicable lessons from it. The conditions of rational calculation are practically never given in practice: time is limited, information is restricted, etc. And yet agents *do* do, much more than if they were behaving randomly, 'the only thing to do.' This is because, following the intuitions of a 'logic of practice' which is the product of a lasting exposure to conditions similar to those which they are placed, they anticipate the necessity immanent in the way of the world. (Bourdieu 1990b: 10–11)

The 'logic of practice' does not so much rely on the explicit statement of rules but more on 'practical wisdom'. Apprenticeship occurs through 'simple familiarization' in which 'the apprentice acquires the principles of the "art" and the art of living' (Bourdieu 1977: 88). 'Habitus is what you have to posit to account for the fact that without being rational, social agents are reasonable' (Bourdieu 1977: 13).

Due to the course of their habitus, agents have dispositions which are regularly exercised in a spontaneous way. There is a tacit normativity – of which the body is the prime site – that governs the social game on which the embodied subject acts. The position of a particular agent is the result of an interplay between a person's habitus and his/her place in a field of positions as defined by the distribution of the appropriate form of capital (be it social, cultural, economic or symbolic) (Bourdieu 1977: 79). Each field is semi-autonomous, characterised by its own agents, its accumulation of history, its own logic of action and its own forms of capital. Fields are not however fully autonomous. Capital is transferable. Each field is immersed in an institutional field of power. There are struggles over the power to define a field.

Ontological Complicity: the Virtuoso

We all participate in the games of our field. However, some people, due to their social trajectory – most especially their class background and scholastic training – are much more inclined to have a sense of the game, as well as the ability to play it. Their social trajectories have immersed them in a habitus that is 'immediately adjusted to the immanent demands of the game'. As Bourdieu aptly puts it, 'they merely need to be what they are in order to be what they have to be' (1990: 11). Specific familial and educational conditions generate dispositions which are in a sense pre-adapted to the demands of a field. Being perfectly adapted to the field, they take up the position of a 'virtuoso', whose 'habitus entertains with the social world which has produced it a real ontological complicity, the source of cognition without consciousness, intentionality without intention, and a practical mastery of the world's regularities which allow one to anticipate the future without even needing to posit it as such' (Bourdieu 1990: 10–11).

The degree to which one has 'ontological complicity' with the demands of the field one works in affects one's 'feel for the game' as well as one's ability to play and partake in it comfortably. Those who are close to the figure of the 'virtuoso' play the game with ease, grace, assurance, familiarity and cadence. Their habitus is rhythmised to the flows of the field. The experience of ontological complicity is thus one:

> when habitus encounters a social world of which it is the product, it is like a 'fish in water'. It does not feel the weight of the water, and it takes the world about itself for granted ... the world encompasses me (*me comprend*) but I comprehend it (*je le comprends*) precisely *because* it has produced the

categories of thought that I apply to it, that it appears to me as self-evident. (Bourdieu and Wacquant 2002: 127–8)

Those who are immediately adapted to the demands of the game have a kinetic mastery of the space within which they operate. Due to the fact that the most elemental 'feel for the game' is an embodied form of knowledge and skills that operate beneath the level of conscious discourse, they have an incarnate sense that arises from the synchrony between their habitus, its social trajectory and the institutional space in which they work.

If we link ontological complicity back to the notion of differentiated inclusion, we can then make sense of different position-taking in regard to class, race and gender. The concept of ontological complicity enables us to apply the analysis of intersections to the actual substance through which differentiation is produced. There are some who are totally 'at home' in their particular chosen profession. The demands of the field, in terms of the 'matrix of perceptions, appreciations, and actions' (Bourdieu 1977: 82–2), resemble their family upbringing and/or their educational careers. They are immediately adapted to the game and are like fish in water. Others feel the weight of the water. For them there is habitus mismatch. There are also degrees to which there is ontological complicity. Class is a crucial differentiator, and so are 'race' and gender. Race, class and gender don't simply interact with each other. They can cancel each other out (Parmar 1982, 1990; Brah 1996), and, in fact, one can compensate for the others. For instance, women who enter predominantly male environments with an élite familial or scholastic background will be inclined to have a habitus that allows for a greater degree of ontological complicity than those who have not had the same social trajectory. At the same time, their gender in a predominantly masculine environment puts them out on a limb. The sedimented outfits are exceedingly ill-fitting. Similarly, those racialised minorities who have had an élite background will have a habitus that is much more in keeping with the demands of the field than those who have not been immersed in this environment. This will occur even while they may 'feel the weight' of the whiteness of organisations and, in this respect, will have occasions where they feel like 'fish out of water', while whiteness is invisible to others, male and female.

For our purposes, what is most significant for thinking about how differentiated inclusion works across different spaces is the 'felicitous encounter' with the world when the habitus matches the demands of the field. The felicitousness makes it possible to partake in the networks and alliances that are formed in the workplace, almost unthinkingly and with ease. Participation in the infinitesimal sources of judgement and measurement is second nature. Those women and racialised minorities who carry weight through the bearing of their carriage, in class or educational terms, as internalised history, via the habitus, are clearly at an advantage compared with those who don't.

Familiar Strangers

While women and racialised minorities are still not totally of the world of professions, because it is predominantly white and male, the classed familiarisations have an impact upon how they interact and feel at 'home', as well as how others respond to them. There is no doubt that their bodies are conspicuous and marked as different entities which are noticed and that they are subjected to additional pressures and expectations because of their minority status. The existing scripts make it impossible for them to be identikit clones. At the same time, though, the semblance makes them, on one level, familiar rather than unfamiliar strangers to the rest of the members. They, at least, partially, mirror and clone the self-image of the hegemonic norm. The comportment and dispositions are not quite, but almost, of the somatic norm. Like the colonial subjects who served the Indian civil service that Bhabha studied (discussed in Chapter 6), they are 'almost the same, but not quite' (1994: 89). However, relative to those racialised minorities who don't share these social trajectories, they are able to: (a) feel at ease with themselves in their work environment; and (b) put those around them at ease. As familiar rather than unfamiliar strangers, there is an element of mutual recognition in terms of the bodily hexis as well as social capital. This mutuality is critical to being considered a 'safe pair of hands', entitled to, and to be trusted with, job opportunities.

Those, for instance, from Oxbridge are trusted because they have trodden a familiar trajectory and are thus 'known' and respected entities. In numerous occupations, Oxbridge, still, in itself operates as a title with 'carriage'. It functions as a badge of honour that carries weight. The symbolic power is in addition attached to social capital. The institutional stamp can lead to further endorsements in the workplace as Oxbridge acts as a warranty which opens up a web of networks. The cultural capital of Oxbridge is transposed into social capital. It bears a value that acts as a signal of a set of 'qualities'. Reflecting on his own social trajectory, Raymond Williams noted that, when he entered the army having been a student at Cambridge who had come from a Welsh mining family and 'community', it soon became apparent to him that Cambridge was an 'admission ticket', a 'privilege ticket'. He says, 'Cambridge mattered because it showed I was the right sort of person' (1989: 11). The relationship between the complicity of habitus and field and social capital has immense implications for the opportunities that are made available.

Slowly, those who do not, in Bourdieu's terminology, have the privilege of ontological complicity, who are not 'fish in water', who don't immediately adapt to the demands of the game can, with familiarisation and the sponsorship of advocates, acquire the art of living in their field, and with success. It is practical mastery, rather than some sort of rational bluffer's guide to the game, that enables them to fill some of the gaps in their initial habitus mismatch. Prolonged immersion, as well as supportive nods from here and there, enables success in the higher levels of hierarchies. Complete ontological complicity does not, however, always obtain for outsiders.

Don Quixote Effect

Beverly Skeggs draws on Bourdieu's work to reflect on her sense of not being at one or at home in the academic world. Looking at herself as a Professor in sociology who has come from a working-class family background, she states:

> My capacity to accrue educational and cultural capitals, however, has only increased my sense of marginalization. I am more aware of the 'right' standards and knowledge and also of the judgments made of those who do not fit. I understand the desire to belong, to be normalized, to go unnoticed, not to be judged, but I am also aware of its impossibility. Proximity to the 'right' knowledge and standards does not guarantee acceptance. They just generate more awareness of how 'wrong' your practices, appearance and knowledge actually are. (1997: 15)

Even after years of being immersed in academia and after concurring in its dealings as well as being endorsed by her peers to the position of Professor, Skeggs still continues to, in Bourdieu's phraseology, 'feel the weight of the water'. There is no doubt that she is an insider; it would be disingenuous to deny this. But at the same time she is not totally *of* the academic world. Her ontological complicity is not of the same extent as that of the 'virtuoso'. She is in a similar, although not identical, position to the petit bourgeois that Bourdieu speaks of. He states they have 'to strive for distinction', which 'is the opposite of distinction: firstly because it involves recognition of a lack and the avowal of a self-seeking aspiration, and secondly because, as can easily be seen in the petit bourgeois, consciousness and reflexivity are both cause and symptom of the failure of immediate adaptation to the situation which defines the virtuoso' (1990b: 10–11).

Bourdieu has identified his own position in the academy in France as a class defector (*transfuge*), who occupies the position of an 'oblate' (Bourdieu and Wacquant 2002: 203). He did not immediately adapt to the academic world and in fact his sense of not being a 'virtuoso' fuelled his theory of habitus and field. Being the son of a farmer who later became a postman in the Béarn village of Lasseube, when he arrived at the Ecole Normale Supérieure as a student, Bourdieu 'felt formidably ill-at-ease'. Craig Calhoun and Loïc Wacquant note:

> Bourdieu at the top of his class at the École Normale Supérieure, the central institution for consecration of French intellectuals, yet he never felt the unselfconscious belonging of those born to wealth, cultural pedigree and elite accents ... His sense of bodily insertion into the competitive and insular universe of French academe encouraged his revitalization of the Aristotelian-Thomist notion of habitus. His awareness of what his classmates and teachers did not see because it felt natural to them informed his accounts... (2002)

Even after several years of being steeped in French intellectual life, Bourdieu noted that he continued to have a deep-rooted feeling of being 'a stranger in the intellectual universe' (Bourdieu and Wacquant 2002: 209). Linking his own habitus to the notion of ontological complicity, he remarked:

> I question this world because it questions me, and in a very profound manner, which goes well beyond the mere sentiment of social exclusion: I never feel fully justified as an intellectual, I do not feel 'at home'; I feel like I have to be answerable – to whom, I do not know – for what appears to me to be an unjustifiable privilege. (Cited in footnote 170, Bourdieu and Waquant 2002: 208–9).

Directly addressing the fish analogy in the theoretical thinking of Bourdieu, from the perspective of race as well as gender, Simmonds notes that, as a black female sociologist, 'In this white world I am a fresh water fish that swims in sea water. I feel the weight of the water ... on my body' (1997: 227). What is highlighted by Simmonds is how her black lecturing body is something that is out of place in academia; it is not the normative figure of authority, while it is, of course, the normative figure of pathology, study and spectacle. She is most certainly to some extent, as an academic, *of* the academic world. Thus, without overstating the analogy, she is a fish, but a different kind. While this fish swims, it does so with a heightened sense of being conspicuously out of place. Regardless of how much a racialised body may be steeped in the 'practical mastery' of the airs, graces and academic specialisms of a field, 'race' marks these bodies out in positions of authority (Puwar 2004b). 'Race' positions one to 'feel the weight of the water', however high and mighty one may be in other respects. At the same time, though, we need to keep in mind that the 'other respects' are critical for enabling some semblance of 'home' within the work environment, which in itself is a significant marker of differentiated inclusion. No doubt Skeggs's whiteness and Bourdieu's white masculinity do enable a form of ontological complicity that, on the grounds of 'race', is not available to Simmonds.

The Contortions of Ontological Denial and Naming

> in a racially structured polity, the only people who can find it psycho-
> logically possible to deny the centrality of race are those who are racially
> privileged, for whom race is invisible precisely because the world is
> structured around them ... The fish do not see the water, and whites do
> not see the racial nature of a white polity because it is natural to them, the
> element in which they move.

> Mills, *The Racial Contract*

There is a close relationship between ontological complicity and onto-logical denial. Those who are in whatever regard – race, class, sexuality or gender – fish in water, whose habitus is immediately adjusted to the demands of the field, do not feel the weight of the water, and hence they do not see the tacit normativity of their own specific habitus, which is able to pass as neutral and universal. This position is produced in an environment where the public sphere and institutional narratives of profes-sionalism operate with a deep-seated denial of embodiment. Thus those who attempt to *name* the particular – in terms of gender, race or class – in what passes as universal face the contortions of naming something that is ontologically denied. It entails going against the grain of the accepted institutional narrative which: (a) denies the body; and (b) relies on a myth of sameness. The challenge posed to institutional narratives and to the sense of professional identities makes naming a contradictory process that adds to the tenuous positionality of 'space invaders'.

The Denial of the Body

Implicit in the 'feel for the game' within the professions is the denial of the body. There is a fervent institutional narrative that prides itself on being based on neutral standards that apply across the board to every body. This is a naturalised discourse sedimented in repeated acts of disavowal. Embedded in the ethics of professionalism is the notion that they are driven by principles of fairness and meritocratic judgement. That these universal standards could be premised on very specific, historically located, corporealites is a complete anathema.

Women and racialised minorities also concur in the disavowal of embodiment. Perhaps this is not surprising, given that declaration of oneself as a gendered or racialised member of a group goes against the grain of established norms of professionalism. Thus we need to recognise that the step towards naming oneself as embodied is not made easily. To draw attention to their own bodies is almost to undermine their claim to professionalism. For women, for instance, to even say that they are conscious of themselves as women challenges the firmly established belief that people are seen as individuals. It is contrary to one of the core identities of their profession.

Genies Coming Out

Notwithstanding the differences between organisations, as well as departments within the same institution, in the degree to which the gendered body is denied, there is none the less a tension to be observed in the identity of professions and the embodied nature of existence. The aversion to seeing individuals as other than individuals makes the act of admitting that gender affects identities and experiences a highly complex affair. The denial of the gendered self is so strong that women themselves can find disclosure 'strange'. A woman in the senior civil service reflected on this process:

> We tried, a few years ago, to have a women's network. We had one or two meetings. I mean, it was a bit like sort of genies coming out ... it was the first time the women, senior women in the Treasury, I mean, sort of Grade 7 upwards, met together and we all felt terribly self-conscious about it because

we had never admitted, basically, to being women... And it was quite an extraordinary meeting, the first one... We felt sort of a bit shifty doing it. And then we got quite self-confident about it, and we thought, 'Well, this is all right. We can actually admit that we're different, and talk to each other.' ... I remember back to this ... this extraordinary meeting we had. It was very strange, that meeting, the first time we all met. We felt so embarrassed. It was quite nice, you know, but sort of ... what if somebody catches us doing this? You know! Very strange.

The use of the phrase 'genies coming out' to describe the experience of coming together as women is highly indicative of the degree to which the significance of gender is denied. 'Coming out' is an enormous struggle in an organisation where the saliency of gender is wished away amidst a myth of an imagined community of individuals. The will to repress the embodied nature of the civil service through the assertion of a somatophobic rational subject has been so pervasive that women have repressed their difference. Moreover, women risk being charged with asking for 'special treatment' or even with thwarting equal opportunities if they assert their difference.

Having spent a whole working lifetime in the civil service, the women themselves have a huge amount of investment in the idea of an impartial, disembodied civil service. We have to recognise that these women are élites with vested interests in an organisation that has a strong tendency to deny the gendered nature of the 'individual' upon which it is modelled. This subsequently places them in a contradictory location that is reflected in the ambivalent and tortuous journey of 'genies coming out'. Patricia Walters notes that at the centre of the senior civil service culture is: 'articulated a set of values, rationality and meritocracy, which aim to be constructed in universal terms and from which gender-based qualities or experiences are judged to be absent. This leads to an organizational tendency to suppress gender rather than to incorporate it explicitly into occupational life' (1987: 13).

Naming Race: 'A Politically Sensitive Issue'

The naming of race is an even more burdened affair, as the discrepancy in the legitimacy attached to race and gender is hugely differentiated. The differences between how race and gender operate in institutions is signalled in the processes of naming. The high degree of sensitivity associated with issues to do with race makes it extremely difficult for black staff to speak out about the matter, even if it is on an anonymous basis. Indeed, one black civil servant I contacted for an interview told me that he could not grant me an interview because it was a politically sensitive subject. The characterisation of the experiences of black senior civil servants as 'politically sensitive' is enormously revealing of the precarious and tentative status given to race. Whilst, on the one hand, statements are made and reports are conducted on how to have better equal opportunities for ethnic minorities, on the other hand, the civil service has a culture that is in denial of race at an even more extreme level than of gender. A few very senior female civil servants have felt comfortable enough to publicly state the gendered nature of their institution. People cannot however speak about race with the same sense of ease because there are so few black people at the senior levels, and also because race is almost a taboo subject. It just does not have the same legitimacy as gender.

The discourse of equal opportunities and diversity accepts that the civil service may have perceptions or recruitment procedures that racially discriminate against certain groups, which undoubtedly need correcting, and the civil service has certainly launched some initiatives to rectify this. However, despite the radical posturing of equal opportunities and diversity procedures and statements, underlying these initiatives is the belief in the liberal ideal of an abstract civil servant. This view professes that people are ultimately seen as people, with race having no relevance for how they are treated. This discourse is, as we saw in the above section in relation to gender, a repetition of the denial of embodiment in liberal theories of equality. It insists on the sameness of humanity. Just as Gatens (1996) and others have argued that the assertion of a gender-free subjecthood ultimately imposes one sex as the norm, in relation to race, bell hooks (*sic*) argues that white people 'have a deep emotional investment in the myth of "sameness"' (1992: 167). The myth of sameness denies, in Hazel Carby's words, that 'everyone in this social order has been constructed in our political imagination as a racialised subject' (1992: 193). To repeat Mills, we could say that these non-white staff 'find that race is, paradoxically, both everywhere and nowhere, structuring their lives but not formally recognized in political/moral theory' (1997: 76).

Seeing Masculinity and Denying Whiteness

Winston Churchill underwent a moment of ontological anxiety when the first woman entered the House of Commons (see Chapter 2). The institution and his identity were, for him, threatened by a female presence. This encounter classically made the invisible – masculinity – visible. That which is ontologically denied lays bear the grounds on which ontological (masculine) complicity relies.

The male and masculine nature of spaces is often not visible to men, or indeed to some women. It is commonly assumed that spaces, languages, positions or structures are neutral. Feminists have had to undo this camouflage, to show that we have male spaces, structures and languages, and that much of this maleness is defined in differentiation to its opposite, the negatively located feminine. Similarly, the racialised nature of white spaces, structures and language is not so easily visible to white people, precisely because whiteness is defined as the norm and the standard neutral space. Both men and women are able to deny their own ontological complicity with whiteness. Though we can now legitimately talk about male spaces, masculine language and so on, it is still not legitimate to talk of whiteness. So, whereas it has become relatively common to hear of the maleness of organisations, the notion of whiteness is still on the margins of academic and public discussions in this field.

Institutional Racism and Whiteness

In the discussions of institutional racism, the 'white male culture' has only very recently been named as an obstacle to promotion. The majority of antiracist initiatives still, however, focus on 'ethnic minorities'. Much of the public discourse of equal opportunities continues to be framed in terms of looking at ethnic 'others'. As the cultures of organisations are naturalised as normal and ordinary, the culture of whiteness is not seen. Being placed as neutral, the norm and the standard, it has not been problematised as being structured by normative whiteness. After all, as Richard Dyer points out, whiteness is defined as having no content 'Having no content, we can't see that we have anything that accounts for our position of privilege and power. This is itself crucial to the security with which we occupy that position' (1997: 9). Thus he states, in order to see whiteness, 'White people need to learn to see themselves as white, to see their particularity. In other words whiteness needs to be made strange.' He argues that the very 'point of looking at whiteness is to dislodge it from its centrality and authority' (1997: 10).

The task of making whiteness visible is an extremely difficult one. It means training the eye to see the racial nature of that which has been defined as outside race, to be unmarked by race, as just normal. We need to recognise how whiteness is embedded in the institutional cultures. In light of the Steven Lawrence Inquiry, the MacPherson Report (1999) and the public discussion of institutional racism which followed, along with the Race Relations Amendment (2000), one would think that it would be absolutely imperative to talk about the whiteness of British institutions. But this has not been the case so far. There has been a resistance to extending the MacPherson analysis of institutional racism in the police force to other parts of the British establishment. Paul Gilroy has noted that:

> To follow that path away from Eltham and to carry the same type of analysis into the corridors of Whitehall, the Inner Temple or the White City is dismissed defensively as manifestly stupid or in quieter tones as a disproportionate reaction. Nobody seems inclined to acknowledge the ways in which race-thinking has shaped the wider common assumptions of the political culture – its premium identities; its shifting sense of nationality; its idea of belonging, of progress, of democracy and, indeed, of history. (1999: unpaginated preface)

Liberalism has what Gilroy points out to be a 'deeply ambivalent relation to the idea of "race"', whose 'precious idea of universal humanity' has excluded black bodies 'from its inner circle on raciological grounds' (1999: 10–11). At the same time, there is a racist subtext underlying the nationalistic euphoria of British electioneering. Viewed as a subject that is politically risqué, parties do not want to come out and take a positive and loud stand against racism.

The Myth of Sameness

There is a collective aversion to recognising and confronting racism. Instead of dealing with racial tension, the liberal ideology of colour-blindness perpetuates the thinking that race does not matter and colour does not make a difference, that we are all the same – one happy human race. Thus racism becomes invisible in a world that professes to be colour-blind. Williams forewarns us against this rather naïve attitude; as she says, it indulges in the:

> false luxury of a prematurely imagined community [based on] the facile innocence of those three notorious monkeys, Hear no evil, See no evil, and Speak no evil. Theirs is a purity achieved through ignorance. Ours must be a world in which we know each other better.

To put it another way, it is a dangerous if comprehensible temptation to imagine inclusiveness by imagining away any obstacles. It is in this way that the moral high ground of good intentions knows its limits. We must be careful not to allow our intentions to verge into outright projection by substituting a fantasy of global seamlessness that is blinding rather than just colour-blind. (1997b: 3–4)

The systemic fantasy of imagined inclusiveness makes it difficult to see racism. People are reluctant to confront the uncomfortable fact that racism is endemic to organisations and professions. The denial of racism places emotional and psychological pressure on black people in public institutions. Williams eloquently expresses the ruptures caused within black psyches who have to coexist in institutions that do not want to see, hear or talk about racism. She says that:

the ability to be one person rather than two refers to some resolution of the ethically dangerous position of one who finds oneself split between the one one is, and the one one feels one *has* to be. The sheltered self and the masquerade.

A black lawyer friend of mine describes a situation that I think exemplifies this split: when her firm first hired her, all the new associates were taken to lunch at an exclusive private club that had until only shortly before barred blacks, Jews and women as members. She found herself the only black person seated at the table while all the servers were black. She found herself on what she called a 'razor's edge' of social consciousness – she was supposed to be enjoying the fruits of her professional success; she was, she knew, supposed to display some subtle mixture of wit, grace and gratitude. Yet sitting at that table engaged in conversation about corporate mergers while acknowledging 'the help' only by quiet sway of her body from right to left as the plates came and went, felt to her like 'ignoring my family,' as she put it.

For black people, the systemic, often nonsensical denial of racial experiences engenders a sense of split identity attending that which is obvious but inexpressible; an assimilative tyranny of neutrality as self-erasure. It creates an environment in which one cannot escape the clanging symbolism of oneself. This is heightened by contrast to all the silent, shifty discomfort of suffering condescension. There's that clunky social box, larger than your body, taking up all that space. You need two chairs at the table, one for you, one for your blackness. (1997b: 25)

In the quest for an 'imagined community', racism becomes what Williams calls a 'public secret' to be discussed in hush-hush tones (1997b: 10). It constitutes a matter that should not be mentioned for fear of opening up the ever-present but often repressed racial fissures that society is inflected with. It is as if 'talking about it will only make things worse' (1997b: 8). We have the 'phenomenon of closeting race [whereby] race matters are resented and repressed in much the same way as matters of sex and scandal: the subject is considered a rude and transgressive one in mixed company, a matter whose observation is sometimes inevitable, but about which, once seen, little should be heard none the less' (Williams 1997b: 6).

Renegade Acts

Speaking out against one's profession is always a risky business, as Bourdieu discovered when he laid the prestige and status structures of the academy bare in his book *Homo Academicus*. There was a barrage of criticism waiting for him, and this was precisely because he had turned his analytical eye on to his own occupational kinfolk. He mentions that 'It is well known that no groups love an "informer", especially perhaps when the transgressor or traitor can claim to share in their own highest values.' A bit like Li Zhi, a renegade mandarin, who titled his text *A Book for Burning* because it revealed the rules of the mandarins' game, by 'divulging tribal secrets' of the tacit norms in academia Bourdieu had revealed the most intimate details of the profession. In these circumstances, he states: 'The sorcerer's apprentice who takes the risk of looking into native sorcery and its fetishes, instead of departing to seek in tropical climes the comforting charms of exotic magic, must expect to see turned against him the violence he has unleashed' (2001: 5).

In seeking to uncover the institutional narratives and myths that glue professional collectivities, one generates a risky positionality, whereby one is seen to be breaking rank. This is an act that goes against the 'practical sense' and the 'feel for the game' by naming the tacitly normative. For space invaders, who never fully belong in the first place, the perils of naming what is ontologically denied in the very being of institutional narratives is even higher. These renegade acts further mark already marked bodies.

Those who come out and speak of racism among their colleagues, in academia, the art world, the civil service or the police, risk being labelled as unprofessional, uncollegiate, confrontational troublemakers. With collegiate support and patronage as fundamental features of working relations, those who are brave enough to speak of racism amongst their ranks have to be prepared to interrogate and perhaps even break links with those one has formed working, dependent and 'chummy' relations.

Thus, within institutions, the aversion to seeing racism is coupled with the aversion to confronting colleagues and especially superiors. There is an overriding preference for consensus, which manifests itself as etiquette. The labour involved in trying to get recognition of racism within institutions that think they are beyond race can't be overestimated. The issue has to be forced against the widespread endemic denial of racism, which is reinforced in the chequer-board terrain of networks and mutual endorsement. The tension between institutional narratives that pride themselves on being built on professional impartiality and speaking of the embodied nature of organisations is exacerbated by relations of mutual dependency within webs of cathexis. Thus those who break with these manners could very easily be in the territory of inappropriate behaviour. It is much easier to hush things up, to seek compromise and to turn the other cheek for fear of the whole artifice upon which careers are built coming apart.

Those who form and join 'black' groups risk being branded as extremists and 'race haters' who are inappropriately challenging their own profession – or 'the hand that feeds them'. By joining a separate grouping, they are often blamed for creating divisions. The fact that these escapes exist because of the entrenched inequalities that are disavowed in everyday institutional encounters is conveniently overlooked as the three-monkeys scenario, discussed above, is once again repeated. The irony, of course, is that black staff are, on the one hand, perceived to be totally marked by race, in terms of who they represent and what they represent, but on the other hand, despite the 'SuperVision' of these bodies as racialised, the saliency of race is denied and repressed by the pervasive liberal ideology of colour-blindness and the necessity of professional collegiality.

–8–

In Summation

This book has been concerned with the question: What happens when those embodied differently come to occupy spaces rarely occupied by them? This question could be asked of all spaces. There is a two-way relationship between spaces and bodies, which locates the coexistence of 'different' bodies in specific spaces as 'space invaders': first, over time specific bodies are associated with specific spaces (these could be institutional positions, organisations, neighbourhoods, cities, nations) and, secondly, spaces become marked as territories belonging to particular bodies.

Today, we are in situation where officially women and 'black' people can enter Parliament, the judiciary, the civil service or academia, for instance, as they are not legally barred from these places. Indeed, we are seeing a gradual increase, albeit slow, in the numbers who enter.[1] Simultaneously, though, white male bodies of a specific habitus continue to be the somatic norm. These bodies are valorised as the corporeal presence of political leadership and management.

There is an undeclared white masculine body underlying the universal construction of the enlightenment 'individual'. Critics of the universal ideal human type in Western thought elaborate on the exclusionary some body in the no body of political theory that proclaims to include every body. In the face of a determined effort to disavow the (male) body, critics have insisted that the 'individual' is embodied, and that it is the white male figure, of a changing habitus, who is actually taken as the central point of reference. The successive unveiling of the disembodied human 'individual' by class theorists, feminists and race theorists has collectively revealed the corporeal specificity of the absolute human type. It is against this template, one that is defined in opposition to women and non-whites – after all, these are the relational terms in which masculinity and whiteness are constituted – that women and 'black' people who enter these spaces are measured.

The designation of specific bodies (women and non-whites) as lacking rationality and all that the abstract male type exemplified was historically and conceptually a central feature of the constitution of the political subject. Racialised and gendered discourses on the body occupied an essential place in the construction of citizenship and political subjecthood. Women were defined as representing all that the social contract in the political realm sought to exclude, that is, emotion, bodies, nature, particularity and affectivity. Men's bodies, on the other hand, were associated with the fantastic qualities of transcendental rationality and universal leadership. Pateman emphasises the role of bodily distinctions when she states: 'In the patriarchal construction of the difference between masculinity and femininity, women lack the capacities necessary for political life. 'The disorder of women' means that they pose a threat to political order and so must be excluded from the public world' (1995: 4).

Charles Mills highlights how the colonial project simultaneously racialised personhood, so that non-whites were perceived as subhuman and not worthy of the social contract. He writes: 'the Racial Contract is explicitly predicated on a politics of the body which is related to the body politic through *restrictions* on which bodies are "politic". There are bodies impolitic whose owners are judged incapable of *forming* or fully *entering* into a body politic' (1997: 53).

Un/Marked Bodies

Despite these exclusions that were central to the construction of the European sovereign subject, enlightenment thought is able to successfully claim that all bodies are the same precisely because whiteness and masculinity can occupy the privileged position of being unmarked by their bodily natures and desires. Definitions of masculinity and whiteness, however, are constructed as negations of what women and non-whites symbolise. It is, after all, women and non-whites who represent the negative side of the binaries of nature/culture, body/mind, affectivity/rationality, subjectivity/objectivity and particularity/universality. Conversely, because somatophobia is central to the definition of whiteness and maleness, both of these identities are defined as an absence of the bodily, a transcendence of the bodily into the realm of rationality, culture and enlightenment.

Within the logic of racial marking, 'others' are known and made visible in a limited sense. In other words, they are racially stereotyped so that they are visible as 'black' bodies, while simultaneously being deemed invisible outside restricted ethnicised confines. Even though the particular taxonomic clustering of phenotypical features with social characteristics shift through time and place, within these stereotypes, non-white bodies are, by and large, associated with the negative side of the binaries discussed above. In a racial polity, their black bodies signify states of uncivilisation and backwardness. The effect of the simultaneous enactment of visibility and invisibility of black bodies is such that 'Race hides those it is projected to mark and illuminates those it leaves unmarked' (Goldberg 1997: 80). Taking gender and race together, we have a complicated and enmeshed layering of 'othering', whereby different bodies are 'othered' according to one criterion or another in relation to the centrifugal invisible somatic norm. This social process enables whites, and most especially white men, those who are unmarked and yet illuminated as 'the norm of humanity', to masquerade as the 'ghosts of modernity' (Goldberg 1997: 83).

While equality is now formally in place, informally personhood is still racialised and gendered. Thus non-whites continue to be associated with nature, particularism and tradition. Whiteness, on the other hand, is heir to everything that non-white bodies lack (Mercer 1995). These non-white bodies are not the most suitable and ideal occupants for positions exalted as being the absolute apex of European civilisation and all that it exemplifies. Like women, they also are 'space invaders', with the difference being that there have been even fewer black bodies in these positions. Also, the positioning of 'black' bodies is even more precarious than that of white female bodies, providing a strong example of 'matter out of place' (c.f. Douglas 1991; Cresswell 1999).

A Collision of Scripts

The naturalised relationship between bodies and spaces has been absolutely crucial to the way I have answered the question: What happens when those embodied differently come to occupy positions rarely or never occupied by someone of that gender and race? I have stated that the sedimented marking of spaces and bodies means that, when women and 'black' bodies actually enter senior positions, this movement represents a collision. Due to the isomorphic relationship between white male bodies and these spaces, whereby these spaces have been defined in opposition to what these 'other' bodies are seen to represent, there is a spatial and bodily collision of imaginations. Female *vis à vis* male and black *vis à vis* white bodies are situated in two diametrically opposed positions, with one being defined in relation to, but to the exclusion of, the other. So masculinity is defined in relation to femininity, but it constitutes what femininity is not. Similarly whiteness is constituted in opposition to what is seen to be racial 'otherness'. As matter out of place, black female bodies create a collision. To adapt a phrase from Edward Said, we could say that the coming together of two identities defined in opposition to each other in black and/or female bodies is tantamount to being in a 'state of civil war'.[2] So, even though female or 'black' bodies physically transgress traditional boundaries by occupying positions of reason and universality, they are still imagined as bearing the traces of 'other' scripts. Their presence in privileged positions in the public realm brings together mutually exclusive scripts.

Disorientation

As matter out of place, the 'space invader' status of these 'different' bodies highlights how privileged positions have historically been 'reserved' for specific kinds of bodies. Their presence also problematises the liberal assertion that bodies do not matter and that positions are constituted in neutered, neutral, colourless terms. The fact that their bodies are noticed as women and/or non-white bodies points towards the embodied nature of these positions. Because authority is imagined in gendered and racialised terms, there is an element of surprise associated with seeing people who are assumed to belong elsewhere. Their presence disrupts and disorientates expectations. Not expecting the occupant of these positions to be 'different', people can be thrown, or their existence induces a 'double take'. Hence, in one sense, their presence represents a discordant event. Being the unexpected, they are often infantilised and assumed to be much more junior than they actually are. There is a resistance to bestowing authority on bodies that do not quite belong.

Amplification of Numbers

Being 'different' from the norm, the bodies of women and non-whites are highly visible. As marked bodies, they undergo double exposure. This can often mean that their numbers become amplified, so that a sprinkling of women or 'black' bodies, especially if they are physically situated together, can be exaggerated. A small presence can represent a territorial threat, with associated metaphors of war, battle and invasion. A tiny number of women can, for instance, be imagined as a 'monstrous regiment of women' that is 'swamping' the 'natural' character of the institutional landscape. This protectionist attitude to space has parallels with wider political discourses on race and immigration. Like immigration, there is a great emphasis on numbers, alongside a moral panic of lowering standards and being 'swamped' by alien 'others'. In this atmosphere, an anxiety that borders on the paranoiac unleashes over-surveillance of any informal or formal gatherings constituted by women or 'black' staff. The fear of losing the unnamed normativity of whiteness and masculinity in organisations is projected on to these other bodies as an 'organisational terror'. Thus the fraternal cathexis of whiteness and masculinity remains invisible, while marked bodies become visible as a psychosomatic 'invasion', especially when they form autonomous collectivities.

Super-Surveillance

Although visibility can be an advantage for being noticed and remembered in organisations where being seen and being known are absolutely crucial for success, it is a double-edged sword. Despite the enlightenment assumption that the body vanishes when reason enters the public realm, it is quite clear that bodies do matter. As 'space invaders', these 'other' bodies are highly visible as sexed and racialised bodies (and it is only the body of the white male that has managed to enjoy the privilege of being invisible). Not being the natural occupants of these positions, these 'different' bodies, as MPs, academics, lawyers, civil servants and artists, are in spaces where they do not belong. In some senses they are aliens in territories they are not meant to be in. Consequently their every gesture, movement and utterance is observed. Viewed suspiciously, they are under Super-Surveillance. There is an element of doubt associated with their coexistence in these spaces. They are not automatically expected to embody the relevant competences. It is assumed that they will not be able to 'do' the scripts as well as the 'normal' 'ordinary' members can. Hence, in order to excel, they have to work against their invisibility and assert their visibility. Being considered as lacking, they have to work, as is often noted, twice as hard to be accepted. In fact, they almost have to display exaggerated forms of competencies to be seen as capable. Existing under a spotlight, minor mistakes are more likely to be noticed and amplified, all of which can lead to authority being easily misplaced in these different bodies. Thus women and non-white staff are at greater risk of being labelled incompetent. Knowing that any mistakes they make can be seen to be expressive of their gender or race, they carry a burden of representation.

MPs are not only under the spotlight of their colleagues and the public but also the media, who can often make or break a politician. For instance, black MPs are very conscious of what they say on race matters because they know that the media watch them for signs of what they consider to be racial extremism. They also have to be aware of the media's criminalising gaze.

Strait-jacketed

In the quest to be accepted as capable and competent as the 'natural' occupants, women and racialised minorities have to work against the pressure of a burden of doubt. This entails a struggle to be seen as not being what negative stereotypical categorisations suggest. However, the attempt to be seen beyond existing imaginary boundaries can prove to be an uphill struggle. Even though women and Black and Asian people have managed to enter spaces they are not expected to occupy, once they are in, they can be placed in spaces that bear some resemblance to stereotypical racial and gendered scripts. So, whilst their movement into these élite positions disrupts traditional boundaries, old boundaries can be reintroduced within the parameters of these spaces. The most obvious case of this is when spaces are made for racialised staff in 'ethnic slots'. Their speech is seen to be tied and locked into their 'race'. And women are granted portfolios associated with the familial private sphere. Those women MPs who then enter heavily masculinised roles, such as defence or agriculture, are easily labelled as lacking. They are, after all, the inappropriate bearers of this specific sort of authority. It is interesting how the territorial departments, such as those connected with arms and land, continue to be spaces that are particularly guarded as male spaces regarded as being 'ill-fitting' for women.

Pateman (1995) points out that the political costume has been constructed with men in mind. In other words, positions of political authority have been constituted in male terms: hence the dissonance when women try to don the same cloak. This cloak is even more ill-fitting for black bodies than it is for white women. After all, as noted earlier, 'black' bodies are not considered to be capable of representing the universal type (Mills 1997). Hence 'black' professionals are constantly trying to be seen beyond the strait-jacket of their 'blackness', as being more than black community leaders or representatives and spokespersons of 'their race'. The struggle to be allowed into 'mainstream' positions is thus relentless.

All of this suggests that the symbiotic relationship between race, gender and positions of authority cannot be overestimated. The gendered and racial symbolism of these positions must be underscored in order to fully appreciate the dynamics involved in the presence of 'newcomers' to particular professions.

Imagining Authority

Irigaray (1985b) has asserted that women are 'symbolically homeless'. Taking masculinity, like femininity, to be socially constituted, rather than as an expression of some inner, gendered, core identity, we can understand masculinity as a performance that requires repetition (Butler 1997b). Such a perspective helps us to see the maleness of the state as an ongoing performative accomplishment. Thus the masculine bias of the state is not a characteristic of the state that is predetermined (Brown 1995). Rather, it requires the repetition of a series of acts that are renewed and consolidated through time. These acts take place in the structural context of a legacy of sedimented masculine rituals. The occupational scripts have been performed as highly masculinist acts. Institutionally organised on the basis of hierarchical fraternising and competitive individualistic exhibitionism, gangs, blocks and allegiances are formed to offer support in a system of patronage and combat (Gasset 1961). Although displays of masculinity in the House of Commons are conducted in a much more spectacular, exaggerated and theatrical manner than in other institutions, exhibitionism and display are underscored by a bureaucratic form of violence across organisations. Needless to say, the hero of these performances is a white male, usually displaying a style of speech and manner of the upper/middle classes. As this is the norm, this is the template against which the speech, gestures and movements of female and black bodies are measured.

However, the paradox facing these 'newcomers' is that the characteristics and ways of being a professional are not free-floating parts of scripts that can be easily donned and enacted by anyone. These gestures, movements and speech patterns belong to whiteness and masculinity. Yet, at the same time, there is an assimilative pressure to conform to the standards and values set by the template. This raises the question: How do female, Black and Asian bodies display attributes that are not traditionally associated with them, but are defined as being core features of the occupational scripts? This dilemma involves managing one's blackness and femininity. Each of these management processes entails different sorts of tensions and demands.

Managing Femininity

While performing in a male outfit, at the same time, women are under pressure to retain their so-called femininity. Given that masculinity is defined in opposition to femininity, the articulation of both types of gender acts within female bodies can prove to be quite a difficult balancing act.

With femininity naturalised as expressive of some inner-core gendered identity, if women do not display the accepted feminine style in these incredibly gendered environments, they risk being labelled as somewhat strange and grotesque (Arthurs and Grimshaw 1999). And certainly, if women want to be accepted in a world that adheres to strict gender fictions, they have to display the acceptable face of femininity. Otherwise, they could alienate their colleagues and be ostracised from the very community they want to have an impact on. This means that they cannot simply don the male costume and mimic the male performance, because then they will be charged with lacking femininity. Thus, unlike men, they cannot totally clone their male leaders. Whilst adhering to the social rules of femininity, at the same time, they have to make sure that they are not too feminine. An excess of femininity could result in them being labelled as hysterical. Located in an organisation based on a masculine performance, a finely balanced fusion of femininity and masculinity has to be enacted.

Margaret Thatcher represented one such combination: the so-called 'iron lady' fused an ultra-feminine appearance (skirts, pearls, blouses, shoes, etc.) with an exaggerated masculine, nationalistic and imperial style of behaviour. She grafted an austere 'ladylike' manner, while at the same time sharing the concerns of the household budget with 'ordinary' wives and mothers, on to a hard and tough male political style. Both Winston Churchill and Britannia constituted Thatcher's particular coat of arms. With the bodies and sexuality of women under super-exposure, how women style their bodies seems to be of immense importance. They are under pressure to reproduce gender differences through reified forms of bodily styles of dress: hence the emphasis on an acceptable form of feminine appearance. The bodies of women MPs are under the gaze of their colleagues, who are not exactly averse to making sexist comments on women's appearance. As spin-doctors and the visual media become more and more important in an iconoclastic age of politics, the pressure is unlikely to decline.

Exclusion of the Private

The bodies of women are a liability. Whilst they are under duress to reiterate differences between masculine and feminine styles through their bodily management, on another level they also have to erase any differences. As objects of display, women's bodies are highly visible, but at the same time they are ignored and kept out of the public sphere. Childbearing and child-rearing have been constructed out of the working practices of Parliament. It is particularly difficult for mothers to be active mothers in the so-called mother of Parliaments. Time is structured on the basis of a one-dimensional public man. The spillover between work and social life makes it very difficult to go against this timing, especially when patronage is an implicit part of working relationships. Thus those women who enter these man-made positions are under pressure to adopt the male life pattern. Instead of relying on the services of a traditional wife, they, like other professional women, buy the time of other women as carers, nannies and housekeepers.

Whether the presence of a greater number of women will shift the policy agenda so that the needs of the domestic sphere and the bodies of women are given serious consideration takes us to that often repeated question: Do different bodies make a difference to policy? Those women MPs who have tried to introduce the bodies of women on to the political agenda have often found that at these moments their own bodies are super-exposed. As a form of male resistance to change, the bodies of the women MPs themselves are subject to scrutiny and ridicule through cheap jibes in the Chamber as well as the media.

We cannot assume that the entry and presence of women in male spaces will 'feminise' these places. This would presume that women are a homogeneous grouping that can generate a mimetic politics from their shared experiences. Moreover, because the historical presence of men in élite positions of the state has become embedded in the institutional practices of these places, wider institutional changes are needed.

Equal to Be the Same ... At Best

Like women, non-white people are also symbolically homeless in the senior positions. Positions of authority have a racial symbolism. The representatives of modernity are unracialised people and, because black people are racially marked, it is not easy for them to be the representatives of humanity. If we understand racial identities, like gender identities, to be constituted through a series of ritualised performances, then we can also talk about whiteness and blackness as performative accomplishments. Although there is a tendency within academia to interpret those who use the phrases whites, whiteness, blacks, blackness and non-whites as articulating essentialist notions of race, I want to stress that the recent move in critical race theory towards discussions of whiteness do not see racial identities as being expressive of some inner essence. This is by no means a sociobiological argument that assumes a determinate relationship between skin colour and behaviour (Carby 1992; hooks 1992; Allen 1994; Mercer 1995; Dyer 1997; Frankenberg 1997; Goldberg 1997; Hill 1997; Kincheloe 1998; Lipsitz 1998). This perspective does, however, attach importance to the signifying consequences of phenotypical features, such as skin colour.

As I noted above, existing gendered scripts place pressure on women to emphasise their physical difference from men in the stylisation of their bodies. In contrast, in relation to ethnicity or race, physical difference in terms of dress or bodily gestures is often much less likely to be accepted. Assimilation is encouraged. In fact, it is often an unspoken requirement of entry into these extremely white spaces. Also, as black bodies are marked out as 'different' and as 'other' in a negative way, they are actually under pressure to minimise any signs of cultural difference. At best, they are equal to be the same. If they want to be accepted they have to deny or erase their cultural difference. Whilst they have to accept that skin colour is a permanent feature of their bodily appearance, they can change or slowly 'whitewash' bodily gestures, social interests, value systems and speech patterns. I should also mention that there is a phenomenon whereby some aspects of cultural difference are celebrated as exotic reifications (Brah 1996; Chow 2002). This form of appreciation is more often than not laced with multicultural orientalism than with an acceptance of open-ended difference (Gunew 1993).

The point I want to underline is that, although 'black' bodies in predominantly white spaces are incredibly visible as different, they are also under assimilative pressure to conform to the behavioural norm. They are expected to take on the ways and means (social codes) of upper/middle class whiteness. Adherence to the norms and values of this hegemonic culture is almost a condition of entry. Those who are able to speak what Bourdieu (1992) has referred to as the 'legitimate state language' and what Fanon (1986) has termed the 'imperial mother language' are more likely to be allowed into 'civilised spaces'. Language is an important distinguishing feature of measurement. It acts as a boundary marker. Those black bodies who speak the imperial/legitimate language are more likely to be heard than those who don't. Indeed, the symbolic power of the imperial/legitimate language can be a source of 'social capital' for those whose racial marking places them as being symbolically lacking (Bourdieu 1990a). Thus 'honorary citizenship' can be granted to those who exhibit signs of so called 'civilisation' and cultural refinement. The performance of what one 'black' civil servant in an interview with me referred to as the 'soft things' (dress, speech, style of interacting) is important for making careers. The display of appropriate behaviour facilitates social interactions that grant visibility in the right places and with the right people. These subtle codes are signs of the discriminating practices through which the exclusivity of these social spaces is constituted. As forms of social measurements they are vital to the formation and reproduction of social boundaries.

The performance of 'soft things' in a manner that has historically been associated with white male bodies does represent a 'menace' to the naturalised relationship between cultural practices and white male bodies. The rupture caused by mimicry, referred to by Bhabha (1994) as the right words in the wrong mouths, can be extremely disorientating to the natural state of affairs, and this really ought not to be underestimated. This 'menace', however, is not menacing enough since it does not problematise the assimilative pressure to mimic the hegemonic culture in the first place. It does not displace the centrifugal place of the culture of whiteness, as it invites others to be equal to be the same. Undeniably, masquerade, parody and rescripting allow for the possibility of subversive scripts. This subversion, however, is always articulated within strictly defined boundaries. Indeed, if the performances were too subversive, they would simply be unacceptable and people would lose out in promotion and opportunities, as they would be considered too strange and unfamiliar.

It is important to note that within these places there is very little space for those who do not want to undergo self-erasure and conform to the cultural norm. For instance, what do people from a working-class background do in these circumstances? If they have spent a long time in education, especially in the élite institutions like Oxbridge, they will have, as pointed out by Bourdieu, become acculturated to the acceptable, respectable language and habitus. Thus they have a form of symbolic and cultural capital. But what about those who do not want to be in a constant state of what Bourdieu has termed 'hyper correction' and actually want to be able to bring their working-class family experiences into what are, metaphorically speaking, white upper/middle-class front rooms? In these circumstances, extending to race a phrase used by Gatens (1996) in relation to gender, the 'cost' of coexistence is erasure or, in other words, as Fanon (1986) says, become white or disappear.

The presence of women and black people in these positions does represent a 'menace,' as it allows for the possibility of imagining professional spaces differently (Phillips 1998). None the less, the presence of different bodies is not enough in itself for transforming the hegemonically placed masculinist customs, rituals and ways and means. Although some female and male MPs, for instance, are problematising the timing and working practices of the House of Commons on the grounds of efficiency, whether and when these demands will be recognised are quite a different manner. Moreover, because many of these customs and rituals are symbols of nationality as well as masculinity, many of the women MPs also have investments in them. Some of them are in fact attached to these ever so British archaic practices, as they give them a sense of national identity. This is a clear sign that women have multi-layered conflicting identities, warning us against assuming a universal women's politics. Moreover, women are themselves differentiated along the lines of several axes (Brah 1996; Parmar 1990), and consequently they have not simply been excluded but have been included differently. This runs through the formation of states, empire and citizenships. There has been a series of identifications and dis-identifications which women have been implicated in.

Becoming Insiders

It has become commonplace to speak of intersections of race, gender and class. However, the complicated processes where outsiders are simultaneously insiders have not been explored in depth. All professionals concur in the social relations and power hierarchies that form the chequer-board terrain of careers. Admittedly they concur to different degrees. They partake in practices of mutual endorsement as well as having different levels of ontological complicity. White women, for instance, are on the grounds of their whiteness, in Bourdieu's terms, 'fish in water': they don't feel the weight of the water. But they do feel the weight of normative masculinity or class.

All successful employees rely on endorsements. For 'different' bodies, who are not part of the 'natural' habitat, sponsors, mentors and advocates are crucial to the promotion of female and black people into élite positions. They often act as facilitators for the entry of these 'alien' bodies. As advocates are often 'trusted' notables in the organisation, insiders are more likely to accept someone who has been endorsed by a colleague whose word they can trust. In a culture where it is important to be visible and known, the patronage of these mentors can be crucial for success. Anomalous bodies can to some extent seem much more amenable if respected notables have endorsed them. The word of some advocates carries more weight than that of others. Institutional trajectories also function as weight, as symbolic, social and cultural capital. Oxbridge, for instance, acts as a badge of honour and approval. Those minorities who carry this weight are certainly more likely to be accepted in 'civilised' spaces that those who don't. They are the familiar strangers likely to be selected in the sifting and sorting that constitutes recruitment procedures. Herein lies the tendency of social cloning within institutions, where those who are alike in social background and theoretical and bodily style are more likely to be endorsed and supported.

Thinking in Bourdieu's terms, specific social trajectories, familial, educational and occupational, furnish bodies with the desired habitus and art of living that is required in privileged positions. Having the right bodily hexis enables manoeuvres to be executed with ease and cadence. Thus a 'feel for the game' provides an advantage. All professionals acquire a 'practical sense' of their field; they have to exist and function. However, some have the advantage of being automatically adjusted to the immanent demands of the field. Others attain it with ambivalence and never obtain the position of the 'virtuoso'. Even if those from working-class backgrounds or women and racialised groups do make it to the apex of organisations, they will rarely have complete 'ontological complicity'. Lacking in class, whiteness or masculinity, they will in one respect or another 'feel like fish out of water'. And the Don Quixote effect that Bourdieu identifies will mean that they are both *of* and not *of* the world of their professions. However, the extent to which they 'fit in' deserves as much attention as the degrees to which they are located as outsiders.

Making the Invisible Visible

Ontological denial of embodiment is implicit to ontological complicity. It is a part of the game. In order to shift the centrifugal place of masculinity and whiteness in institutional structures and practices, as well as the symbolic imagination of authority, the central place of whiteness and masculinity needs to be named and problematised. Naming, however, can prove to be extremely difficult when institutions disavow cultural and corporeal specificity. Professional institutional liberal narratives have a propensity to deny the invisible centre. The levels of the denial are quite specific to each institution. For instance, the masculinist bias of the House of Commons is much more readily voiced than the masculinist nature of the senior civil service, and the gendered nature of both of these institutions is more likely to be recognised than their racial character. The condition of colour-blindness is much more extensive than gender-blindness. There is a huge amount of resistance within the professions to making the gendered and racial nature of these environments visible. There is a reluctance to face up to how different staff are afforded the advantages of 'ontological complicity'.

The debate between those who emphasise 'difference' and those who stress sameness is at the centre of all struggles to acknowledge the embodied nature of social relations and institutions. The contours of this dispute are repeatedly circulated in debates on the saliency of embodiment and the prematurely imagined community of human sameness. It is extremely difficult to get recognition of the fact that the norm is based on a one-dimensional man and that universal standards are based on a specific culture, when professions think of themselves as being neutral, meritocratic and objective. This representation is deeply ingrained. There is a hegemonic discourse which propounds that all people are plainly treated as 'individuals'. A disavowal of embodiment makes it very difficult for those who are situated as different from the centre to actually name their difference. Admitting difference in an organisation which asserts that everybody is the same and that standards are neutral is more than a troublesome task. After all, it goes against a core identity of being a professional. The difficulty is illustrated by the way in which one of the women in the senior civil service spoke about the experience of women coming together in her department as a group as being a bit like 'genies coming out'. There is a certain amount of trepidation and anxiety attached to 'coming out' visibly as women.

Certainly those outsiders who do not discuss their difference and just try to blend in with the norm are more likely to be accepted and to succeed. As a strategy of survival, then, they might judge it more pragmatic to remain silent and to concentrate on the job. How women position themselves in relation to naming gender is actually an integral part of the management of femininity. Those who are considered to be 'too vocal' on gender issues may be labelled as boisterous, aggressive and hysterical. After all, as 'space invaders', women are in a somewhat tenuous position anyway. This location could be exacerbated by going against the professional work ethic in the naming of gender.

'Black' staff are perhaps even more hesitant to discuss their difference. Race is a highly sensitive, taboo subject, discussed in what Patricia Williams has called 'hush-hush tones'. Even academics, who regularly name the dynamics of 'race' in other organisations, have barely begun to see how their own institutions are racialised. This subject has by no means received as much exposure as has the gender of institutions. It is notable how academics as well as policy-makers have started to see the gender of organisations, but have barely recognised the central place of race in the construction of international, national and local institutions. Gender has much more legitimacy as a social issue in public and policy discourse. In contrast, there is an enormous amount of effort involved in getting recognition of race, because colour-blindness is so endemic to British institutions. Like gender, but with a stronger emphasis, it is asserted that differences should not be mentioned and that we should consider that we are all the same. To do otherwise is seen to be asking for 'special treatment'. In fact, it is asserted by liberal discourses that the marking out of race and gender will only make matters worse. The position taken by 'black' people on race in their organisation is a part of how they manage their blackness in a place they are not expected to be in. Those who take a strong line on race can be seen to be 'too black' and too disruptive for the organisation.

By discussing a taboo subject that is closeted under the veneer of professional neutrality, those who choose to come out and speak against racism amongst their ranks risk being seen as engaged in renegade acts. Divulging the secrets of your own occupational tribe is a risky business indeed, especially when your 'space invader' status already marks you out and grants you a tenuous location. Moreover, it often entails confronting colleagues and seniors, many of whom you need in order simply to exist and function in the hierarchical cathexis of relations that form collectivities in organisations. Thus, acts that name have to be taken strategically and with the support of advocates who carry weight.

Bibliography

Acker, J. (1989), 'The Problem with Patriarchy', *Sociology* 23 (2): 235–40.

Acker, J. (1990), 'Hierarchies, Jobs, Bodies: a Theory of Gendered Organisations', *Gender and Society* 4: 139–58.

Allen, J. (2003), *Lost Geographies of Power*, Oxford: Blackwell Publishing.

Allen, T. (1994), *The Invention of the White Race*, Vol. 1. London: Verso.

Alvesson, M. and Due Billing, Y. (1997), *Understanding Gender and Organization*, London: Sage.

Anderson, B. (1991), *Imagined Communities: Reflections on the Origin and Spread of Nationalism*, London: Verso.

Araeen, R. (1994), *Making Myself Visible*, London: Kala Press.

Araeen, R. (2000), 'The Art of Benevolent Racism', *Third Text* 51: 57–64.

Arthurs, J. and Grimshaw, J. (1999), *Women's Bodies: Discipline and Transgression*, London: Cassell.

Atkinson, A. (1997), *Funny Girls: Cartooning for Equality*, London: Penguin Books.

Back, L. (1994), *New Ethnicities and Urban Culture: Racisms and Multiculture in Young Lives*, London: UCL Press.

Barrett, M. (1997), 'Words and Things: Materialism and Method in Contemporary Feminist Analysis', in S. Kemp and J. Squires (eds), *Feminisms*, Oxford: Oxford University Press.

Bell, V. (1999), *Performativity and Belonging*, Nottingham: TCS, Nottingham Trent University.

Bhabha, H. (1994), *The Location of Culture*, London: Routledge.

Bhabha, H.K. (1998), 'Anish Kapoor: Making Emptiness', in P.L. Tazzi, H. Bhabha and A. Kapoor (eds), *Anish Kapoor*, London: Hayward Gallery and University of California Press.

Bhatia, N. (2003), 'Romantic Transgressions in the Colonial Zone: Reading Mircea Eliade's Bengal Nights and Maitreyi Devi's It Does Not Die', in N. Puwar and P. Raghuram (eds), *South Asian Women in the Diaspora*. Oxford: Berg Publishers.

Bibliography

Bhatt, C. (2002), 'Primordial Being: Enlightenment and the Indian Subject of Postcolonial Theory', in P. Sandford and P. Osborne (eds), *Philosophies of Race and Ethnicity*, London: Continuum.

Bottomore, T. (1993), *Elites and Society*, London: Routledge.

Bourdieu, P. (1958), *Sociologie de l'Algérie*, Paris: Presses Universitaires de France.

Bourdieu, P. (1977), *Outline of a Theory of Practice*, Cambridge: Cambridge University Press.

Bourdieu, P. (1984), *Distinction: a Social Critique of the Judgement of Taste*, London: Routledge & Kegan Paul.

Bourdieu, P. (1990a), *The Logic of Practice*, Cambridge: Polity.

Bourdieu, P. (1990b), *In Other Words: Essays Towards a Reflexive Sociology*, Oxford: Polity.

Bourdieu, P. (1992), *Language and Symbolic Power: the Economy of Linguistic Exchanges*, Cambridge: Polity.

Bourdieu, P. (1995), *The Logic of Practice*, Cambridge: Polity.

Bourdieu, P. (1998), *Practical Reason*, Oxford: Polity Press.

Bourdieu, P. (2001), *Homo Academicus*, Oxford: Polity Press.

Bourdieu, P. and Darbel, A. (1963), *Travail et travailleurs en Algérie*, Paris: Mouton.

Bourdieu, P. and Sayad, A. (1964), *Le Déracinement: la crise de l'agriculture traditionnelle en Algérie*, Paris: Editions de Minuit.

Bourdieu, P. and Wacquant, L. (2002), *An Invitation to Reflexive Sociology*, Chicago: University of Chicago Press.

Brah, A. (1992), 'Difference, Diversity and Differentiation', in J. Donald and A. Rattansi (eds), *'Race', Culture and Difference*, London: Open University/Sage.

Brah, A. (1996), *Cartographies of a Diaspora*, London: Routledge.

Brown, W. (1988), *Manhood and Politics: a Feminist Reading in Political Theory*, Totowa, NJ: Rowman & Littlefield.

Brown, W. (1995), *States of Injury: Power and Freedom in Late Modernity*, Princeton, NJ: Princeton University Press.

Burch, M. and Moran, A. (1985), 'The Changing Political Elite', *Parliamentary Affairs* 38: 1–15.

Burgin, V. (1996), *In/Different Spaces: Place and Memory in Visual Culture*, Berkeley and Los Angeles, California: University of California Press.

Burris, B. (1996), 'Technocracy, Patriarchy and Management', in D. Collinson and J. Hearn (eds), *Men as Managers, Managers as Men*, London: Sage.

Bibliography

Burton, A. (1994), *Burdens of History: British Feminists, Indian Women and Imperial Culture, 1865–1915*, Chapel Hill, NC: University of North Carolina Press.

Butler, J. (1989), *Gender Trouble: Feminism and the Subversion of Identity*, London: Routledge.

Butler, J. (1993a), *Bodies that Matter: On the Discursive Limits of 'Sex'*, London: Routledge.

Butler, J. (1993b), 'Endangered/Endangering: Schematic Racism and White Paranoia', in R. Gooding-Williams (ed.), *Reading Rodney King/Reading Urban Uprising*, London: Routledge.

Butler, J. (1996), 'Gender as Performance', in P. Osborne (ed.), *A Critical Sense*, London: Routledge.

Butler, J. (1997a), *Excitable Speech: a Politics of the Performative*, London: Routledge.

Butler, J. (1997b), 'Performative Acts and Gender Constitution: An Essay in Phenomenology and Feminist Theory', in K. Conboy, N. Medina and S. Stanbury (eds), *Writing on the Body: Female Embodiment and Feminist Theory*, New York: Columbia University Press.

Butler, J. (1999), 'Performativity's Social Magic', in R. Shusterman (ed.), *Bourdieu: a Critical Reader*, Oxford: Blackwell Publishers.

Calhoun, C. and Wacquant, L. (2002), '"Everything is Social": In Memoriam, Pierre Bourdieu (1939–2002)', *Footnotes* 30 (2): www. asnet.org/footnotes/feb02.

Campbell, B. (2003), 'The Revolution Betrayed', *Guardian Weekend Magazine*, London, 11 November 2003.

Carby, H. (1992), 'The Multicultural Wars', in G. Dent (ed.), *Black Popular Culture*, Seattle: Bay Press.

Carter, E., Donald, J. and Squires, J. (1995), *Space and Place: Theories of Identity and Location*, London: Lawrence & Wishart.

Chambers, E. (1999), *Annotations 5. Run Through the Jungle: Selected Writings by Eddie Chambers*, London: Institute of International Visual Arts.

Chambers, I. (1990), *Border Dialogues: Journeys in Postmodernity*, London: Routledge.

Chambers, I. (1994), *Migrancy, Culture, Identity*, London: Routledge.

Chapman, R. and Rutherford, J. (1988), *Male Order: Unwrapping Masculinity*, London: Lawrence & Wishart.

Chaudhuri, N. and Strobel, M. (1992), *Western Women and Imperialism: Complicity and Resistance*, Bloomington and Indianapolis: Indiana University Press.

Childs, S. (2001), 'In Their Own Words: New Women MPs and the Substantive Representation of Women', *British Journal of Politics and International Relations* 3 (2): 173–9.

Chow, R. (1993), *Writing Diaspora*, Bloomington and Indianapolis: Indiana University Press.

Chow, R. (2002), *The Protestant Ethnic and The Spirit of Capitalism*, New York: Columbia University Press.

Cockburn, C. (1987), *Women, Trade Unions and Political Parties*, London: Fabian Society.

Cockburn, C. (1991), *In the Way of Women: Men's Resistance to Sex Equality in Organizations*, Basingstoke: Macmillan Education.

Cohen, P. (1999), 'In Visible Cities: Urban Regeneration and Place-building in the Era of Multicultural Capitalism', *Communal/Plural* 7 (1): 9–28.

Collinson, D. and Hearn, J. (1996), '"Men" at Work: Multiple Masculinities/Multiple Workplaces', in M. Mac an Ghaill (ed.), *Understanding Masculinities*, Buckingham: OUP.

Connell, R. (1987), *Gender and Power: Society, the Person and Sexual Politics*, Cambridge: Polity/Blackwell.

Connell, R. (1995), *Masculinities*, Cambridge, UK: Polity Press.

Cresswell, T. (1999), *In Place/Out of Place: Geography, Ideology and Transgression*, Minneapolis: University of Minnesota Press.

Crompton, R. (1997), *Women and Work in Modern Britain*, Oxford: Oxford University Press.

Crompton, R. and Sanderson, K. (1990), *Gendered Jobs and Social Change*, London: Unwin Hyman.

Daly, M. (1978), *Gyn/Ecology: the Metaethics of Radical Feminism*, London: Women's Press.

Domhoff, G. (1967), *Who Rules America?* Engelwood Cliffs: Prentice-Hall.

Douglas, M. (1991), *Purity and Danger: an Analysis of the Concepts of Pollution and Taboo*, London: Routledge.

DuCille (2001), 'The Occult of True Black Womanhood: Critical Demeanour and Black Feminist Studies', in K. Bhavnani (ed.), *Feminism and Race*, Oxford: Oxford University Press.

Du Bois, W.E.B. (1989), *The Souls of Black Folk*, New York: Bantam.

Du Gay, P. (2000), *In Praise of Bureaucracy*, London: Sage.

Dyer, R. (1997), *Whiteness*, London: Routledge.

Eagle, M., Lovenduski, J. and Fabian Society (1998), *High Time or High Tide for Labour Women?* London: Fabian Society.

Fanon, F. (1986), *Black Skin, White Masks*, London: Pluto.

Bibliography

Fiske, J. (1998), 'Surveilling the City: Whiteness, the Black Man and Democratic Totalitarianism', *Theory, Culture and Society* 15 (2): 67–88.

Foucault, M. (1970), *Discipline and Punish: the Birth of the Prison*, London: Allen Lane.

Frankenberg, R. (1997), *Displacing Whiteness: Essays in Social and Cultural Criticism*, Durham, NC: Duke University Press.

Franzway, S., Court, D. and Connell, R. (1989), *Staking a Claim: Feminism, Bureaucracy and the State*, Oxford: Polity Press.

Gabriel, J. (1998), *Whitewash*, London: Routledge.

Gasset, J. (1961), 'The Sportive Origin of the State', in J. Gasset (ed.), *History as a System and Other Essays toward a Philosophy of History*, New York: Norton.

Gatens, M. (1996), *Imaginary Bodies: Ethics, Power, and Corporeality*, London: Routledge.

Gherardi, S. (1995), *Gender, Symbolism and Organizational Cultures*, London: Sage.

Gibson, N. (2003), *Fanon: the Postcolonial Imagination*, Oxford: Polity.

Gilroy, P. (1987), *'There Ain't No Black in the Union Jack': the Cultural Politics of Race and Nation*, London: Hutchinson.

Gilroy, P. (1993), *The Black Atlantic: Modernity and Double Consciousness*, London: Verso.

Gilroy, P. (1999), *Joined-up Politics and Post-colonial Melancholia*, London: Institute of Contemporary Arts.

Gilroy, P. (2000), *Between Camps*, London: Penguin Books.

Glucksman, M. (2000), *Cottons and Casuals: The Gendered Organisation of Time and Space*, Durham: Sociology Press.

Goldberg, D. (1996), 'In/Visibility and Super/Vision', in L. Gordon, T. Sharpley-Whiting and R. White (eds), *Fanon: A Critical Reader*, Oxford: Blackwell.

Goldberg, D. (1997), *Racial Subjects: Writing on Race in America*, New York: Routledge.

Goldberg, T. (2002), *The Racial State*, Oxford: Blackwell Publishers.

Gooding-Williams, R. (1993), *Reading Rodney King/Reading Urban Uprising*, London: Routledge.

Gordon, L.R. (1995), *Fanon and the Crisis of European Man*, New York: Routledge.

Gormley, A. (1996), *Field for the British Isles*, Llandudno, Wales: Oriel Mostyn.

Grosz, E. (1995), *Space, Time, and Perversion: Essays on the Politics of Bodies*, London: Routledge.

Grosz, E. (1999), 'Bodies-Cities', in J. Price and M. Shildrick (eds), *Feminist Theory and the Body: A Reader*, Edinburgh: Edinburgh University Press.

Grosz, E. (2001), *Architecture From the Outside: Essays on Virtual and Real Space*, Cambridge, Massachusetts: MIT Press.

Gultsman, W. (1963), *The British Political Elite*, London: McGibbon and Kee.

Gunew, S. (1993), 'Against Multiculturalism: Rhetorical Images', in G.L. Clark, D. Forbes and R. Francis (eds), *Multiculturalism, Difference and Postmodernism*, Melbourne: Longman Cheshire.

Hall, C. (1992) *White, Male and Middle Class*, Oxford: Polity.

Hall, S. (1988), *The Hard Road to Renewal: Thatcherism and the Crisis of the Left*, London: Verso.

Hall, S. (1989), 'The Local and the Global', in A. King (ed.), *Culture, Globalization, and the World System: Contemporary Conditions for the Representation of Identity*, Albany: SUNY Press.

Hall, S. (1992), 'The Question of Cultural Identity', in S. Hall, D. Held and T. McGrew (eds), *Modernity and its Futures*, Oxford: Polity Press in association with Blackwell Publishers and the Open University.

Hall, S. (1998), 'Aspiration and Attitude ... Reflections on Black Britain in the Nineties', *New Formations* 33: 38–46.

Hall, S. and Jacques, M. (1983), *The Politics of Thatcherism*, London: Lawrence & Wishart in association with Marxism Today.

Hall, S., Jefferson, T., Clarke, J. and Robert, B. (1977), *Policing the Crisis: Mugging, the State, and Law and Order*, London: Macmillan.

Hardt, M. and Negri, A. (2000), *Empire*, London: Harvard University Press.

Harris, C. (1991), 'Configurations of Racism: The Civil Service, 1945–60', *Race and Class* 33: 1–30.

Hearn, J. (1992), *Men in the Public Eye: the Construction and Decostruction of Public Men and Public Patriarchies*, London: Routledge.

Hearn, J. and Parkin, W. (1987), *'Sex' at 'Work': the Power and Paradox of Organisation and Sexuality*, Brighton: Wheatsheaf.

Hesse, B. (1997) 'White Governmentality: Urbanism, Nationalism, Racism', in S. Westwood and J. Williams (eds) *Imagined Cities*, London: Routledge.

Hesse, B. (1999), 'It's Your World: Discrepant Multiculturalisms', in P. Cohen (ed.), *New Ethnicities, Old Racisms*, London: Zed Books.

Hill, M. (1997), *Whiteness: a Critical Reader*, New York: New York University Press.

Hochschild, A. (2003), *The Managed Heart: the Commercialisation of Human Feeling*, Berkeley, California: University of California Press.

hooks, b. (1991), *Yearning: Race, Gender and Cultural Politics*, London: Turnaround.

hooks, b. (1992), *Black Looks: Race and Representation*, London: Turnaround.

Howe, D. (1988), *Black Sections in the Labour Party*, London: Race Today Publications.

Huet, M. (1982), *Rehearsing the Revolution: The Staging of Marat's Death 1793–1797*, Berkeley: University of California Press.

Irigaray, L. (1992), *Elemental Passions*, London: Athlone Press.

Irigaray, L. (1985a), *Speculum of the Other Woman*, Ithaca: Cornell University Press.

Irigaray, L. (1985b), *The Sex Which is Not One*, Ithaca: Cornell University Press.

Irigaray, L. (2000), *Democracy Begins Between Two*, London: Athlone Press.

Irigaray, L. (2002), *Between East and West: from Singularity to Community*, New York: Columbia University Press.

Itzin, C. and Newman, J. (1996), *Gender, Culture and Organizational Change: Putting Theory into Practice*, London: Routledge.

Kearney, R. (2003), *Strangers, Gods and Monsters*, London: Routledge.

Keith, M. (1993) *Race, Riots and Policing – Lore and Disorder in a Multi-Racist Society*, London: UCL Press.

Keith, M. (1999), 'Identity and the Spaces of Authority', in J. Solomos and L. Back (eds) *Theories of Race and Racism: A Reader*, London: Routledge.

Kellner, D. (1997), 'Critical Theory and Cultural Studies: the Missed Articulation', in J. McGuigan (ed.), *Cultural Methodologies*, London: Sage.

Kincheloe, J.L. (1998), *White Reign: Deploying Whiteness in America*, New York: St Martin's Press.

Kristeva, J. (1980), *Powers of Horror: An Essay on Abjection*, New York: Columbia University Press.

Labour Research (1997), 'A House Fit for Families', *Labour Research*, June.

Landes, J. (1998), 'The Public and Private Sphere Feminism: A Feminist Reconsideration', in J. Landes (ed.), *Feminism, the Public and the Private*, Oxford: Oxford University Press.

Landry, D. and Maclean, G.M. (1995), *The Spivak Reader: Selected Works of Gayatri Chakravorty Spivak*, London: Routledge.

Lawrence, E. (1982), 'In the Abundance of Water the Fool is Thirsty: Sociology and Black "Pathology"', in CCCS (ed.), *The Empire Strikes Back*, London: Hutchinson Education.

Lefebvre, H. (2002), *The Production of Space*, Oxford: Blackwell Publishing.

Lemert, C. (1997), *Social Things*, Lanham, Maryland, USA: Rowman & Littlefield Publishers.

Le Sueur, J. (2001), *Uncivil War: Intellectuals and the Identity Politics During the Decolonization of Algeria*, Forward by Pierre Bourdieu, Philadelphia, Pennsylvania: University of Pennsylvania Press.

Lévi-Strauss, C. (1968), *Structural Anthropology*, Vol. 1, trans. C. Jacobson and B. Gundfest Schoef, London: Allen Lane.

Lipsitz, G. (1998), *The Possessive Investment in Whiteness: How White People Profit from Identity Politics*, Philadelphia: Temple University Press.

Lovell, T. (2002), 'Resisting with Authority: Historical Specificity, Agency and Performative Self'. Paper delivered at International Conference on 'After Bourdieu: Feminists Evaluate Bourdieu, International Perspectives', Manchester University, October.

Lovenduski, J. and Norris, P. (1995) *Political Recruitment*, Cambridge: Cambridge University Press.

Mac an Ghaill, M. (1996), *Understanding Masculinities: Social Relations and Cultural Arenas*, Buckingham: Open University Press.

McClintock, A. (1995), *Imperial Leather*, London: Routledge.

McDougall, L. (1998), *Westminster Women*, London: Vintage.

McDowell, L. (1996), 'Spatializing Feminism: Geographic Perspectives', in N. Duncan (ed.), *Body/Space*, London: Routledge.

McDowell, L. (1997), *Capital Culture: Gender at Work in the City*, Oxford and Malden, MA: Blackwell Publishers.

Macey, D. (2000), *Frantz Fanon: A Life*, London: Granta Books.

Macey, D. (2002), 'Fanon, Phenomenology, Race', in S. Sandford and P. Osborne (eds), *Philosophies of Race and Ethnicity*, London: Continuum.

Mackay, F. (2001), *Love and Politics: Women Politicians and the Ethics of Care*, London: Continuum International Publishing Group.

McNay, L. (2002), 'On Reductionism in Bourdieu and Butler'. Paper delivered at International Conference on 'After Bourdieu: Feminist Evaluate Bourdieu, International Perspectives', Manchester University, October.

MacPherson of Cluny, S.W. (1999), *The Steven Lawrence Inquiry: Report of an Inquiry by William MacPherson of Cluny*, London: HMSO.

Bibliography

McQueen, S. (2002), Public Discussion Organised by *Artangel*, London: Cinema Lumiére, St Martin's Lane.

Maharaj, S. (1999), 'Black Art's Autrebiography', in E. Chambers (ed.), *Annotations* 5, London: International Institute of Visual Arts.

Marshall, J. (1984), *Women Managers: Travellers in a Male World*, Chichester: Wiley.

Marx, K. (1843), *Critique of Hegel's 'Philosophy of Right'*, Cambridge: Cambridge University Press.

Massey, D. (1996), *Space, Place and Gender*, Oxford: Polity Press.

Mercer, K. (1994), *Welcome to the Jungle: New Positions in Black Cultural Studies*, London: Routledge.

Mercer, K. (1995), 'Busy in the Ruins of Wretched Phantasia', in R. Farr (ed.), *Mirage: Enigmas of Race, Difference and Desire*, London: Institute of Contemporary Arts/Institute of International Visual Arts.

Mills, C. (1997), *The Racial Contract*, Ithaca: Cornell University Press.

Mills, C. (1998), *Blackness Visible: Essays on Philosophy and Race*, Ithaca, NY: Cornell University Press.

Mills, C.W. (1963), *Power, Politics, and People: the Collected Essays of C. Wright Mills*, London: Oxford University Press.

Mills, S. (1998), 'Post-Colonial Feminist Theory', in S. Jackson and J. Jones (eds), *Contemporary Feminist Theories*, Edinburgh: Edinburgh University Press.

Mohanty, C. (1988), 'Under Western Eyes: Feminist Scholarship and Colonial Discourses', *Feminist Review* 30: 60–88.

Mookherjee, N. (2003), 'Gendered Embodiments: Mapping the Body-Politic of the Raped Women and the Nation in Bangladesh', in N. Puwar and N. Raghuran (eds), *South Asian Women in the Diaspora*, Oxford: Berg.

Mosca, G. and Livingston, A. (1939), *The Ruling Class*, London: McGraw-Hill.

Moyser, G. and Wagstaffe, M. (1987), *Research Methods for Elite Studies*, London: Allen & Unwin.

Muir, H. (2003), 'When It Comes to Mandela's Statue, It's All in the Hands' *The Guardian*, 10 December.

Nash, C. (1994), 'Remapping the BodyLand: New Cartographies of Identity, Gender, and Landscape in Ireland', in A. Blunt and R. Gillian (eds), *Writing Women and Space: Colonial and Postcolonial Geographies*, New York: Guildford Press.

Nelson, J. (1996), *Feminism, Objectivity and Economics*, London: Routledge.

Bibliography

Nixon, S. (2003), *Creative Cultures: Gender and Creativity at Work in Advertising*, London: Sage.

Norris, P. (ed.) (1995), *Women, Media, and Politics*, New York: Oxford University Press.

Nunn, H. (2002), *Thatcher, Politics and Fantasy*, London: Lawrence & Wishart.

Oakley, A. (1981), 'Interviewing Women: a Contradiction in Terms', in H. Roberts (ed.), *Doing Feminist Research*, London: Routledge & Kegan Paul.

Okin, S. (1992), *Women in Western Political Thought*, Princeton, NJ: Princeton University Press.

Ortner, S. (1974), 'Is Female to Male as Nature is to Culture?', in M. Rosaldo and L. Lamphere (eds), *Women, Culture and Society*, Stanford: Stanford University Press.

Parekh, B. (1995), 'Liberalism and Colonialism: a Critique of Locke and Mill', in J.N. Pieterse and B. Parekh (eds), *The Decolonization of Imagination*, London: Zed Books.

Pareto, V. and Livingston, A. (1935), *The Mind and Society*, London: Cape.

Parker, A., Russo, M., Sommer, D. and Yaeger, P. (1992), *Nationalisms and Sexualities*, New York: Routledge.

Parmar, P. (1982), 'Gender, Race and Class: Asian Women in Resistance', in CCCS (ed.), *The Empire Strikes Back: Race and Racism in 70's Britain*, London: Hutchinson.

Parmar, P. (1990), 'Black Feminism: the Politics of Articulation', in J. Rutherford (ed.), *Identity: Community, Culture, Difference*, London: Lawrence & Wishart.

Pateman, C. (1988), *The Sexual Contract*, Oxford: Polity Press.

Pateman, C. (1995), *The Disorder of Women: Democracy, Feminism and Political Theory*, Cambridge: Polity.

Pateman, C. and Puwar, N. (2002), 'Interview with Carole Pateman: The Sexual Contract, Women in Politics, Globalization and Citizenship', *Feminist Review* 70: 123–33.

Phillips, A. (1993), *Democracy and Difference*, Cambridge: Polity Press.

Phillips, A. (1998) *The Politics of Presence*, Oxford: OUP.

Phillips, M. (1980) *The Divided House: Women at Westminster*, London: Sedgwick & Jackson.

Pitkin, H. (1984), *Fortune is a Woman*, Berkeley: University of California Press.

Probyn, E. (1993), *Sexing the Self: Gendered Positions in Cultural Studies*, London: Routledge.

Putnam, R. (1976), *The Comparative Study of Political Elites*, Englewood Cliffs: Prentice-Hall.

Puwar, N. (1997a), 'Reflections on Interviewing Women Elites', *Sociological Research Online* 2 (1). www.socresonline.org.uk/socresonline/2/1/4.html

Puwar, N. (1997b), 'Gender and Political Elites: Women in the House of Commons', *Sociology Review* 7 (2): 2–4.

Puwar, N. (2000), 'Women in the House (of Commons)', *Politics Review* 10 (1): 15–19.

Puwar, N. (2001), 'The Racialised Somatic Norm and the Senior Civil Service', *Sociology* 35 (3): 651–70.

Puwar, N. (2002), 'Multicultural Fashion ... Stirrings of Another Sense of Aesthetics and Memory', *Feminist Review* 30: 60–88.

Puwar, N. (2003a), 'Parole situate e politica globale', *Derive Approdi* (movimenti postcoloniali) 23: 7–19.

Puwar, N. (2003b), 'Melodramatic Postures and Constructions', in N. Puwar and P. Raghuram (eds) *South Asian Women in the Diaspora*, Oxford: Berg Publishers.

Puwar, N. (2003c), 'Exhibiting Spectacle and Memory', in N. Puwar and N. Bhatia (eds), *Fashion Theory: Special Double Issue on Orientalism* 7 (3/4): 257–74.

Puwar, N. (2004a), 'Speaking Positions in Global Positions', *Multitudes*, article 1321, French translation.

Puwar, N. (2004b), 'The Somatic Norm in Universities: a Cat, Three Monkeys and Fish In/Out of Water', in I. Law, D. Phillips and L. Turney (eds), *Institutional Racism in Higher Education*, Stoke-on-Trent: Trentham Press.

Puwar, N. (2004c), 'Making a Difference?', *British Journal of Politics and International Relations* 6(1): 65–80.

Read, A. (ed.) (1996), *The Fact of Blackness: Frantz Fanon and Visual Representation*, London: Institute of Contemporary Arts/INIVA..

Reskin, B. and Padavic, I. (1994), *Women and Men at Work*. Thousand Oaks: Pine Forge Press.

Rich, P. (1989), *Race and Empire in British Politics*, Cambridge: Cambridge University Press.

Riviere, J. (1986), 'Womanliness as a Masquerade', in V. Burgin, J. Donald and C. Kaplan (eds), *Formations of Fantasy*, London: Methuen.

Robbins, D. (2000), *Pierre Bourdieu*, London: Sage.

Roper, M. (1993), *Masculinity and the British Organization Man since 1945*, Oxford: Oxford University Press.

Said, E. (1994a), *Culture and Imperialism*, London: Vintage.

Said, E. (1994b), *Representations of the Intellectual: the 1993 Reith Lectures*, London: Vintage.

Said, E. (1995), *Orientalism*, Harmondsworth: Penguin.

Said, E. (1999), *Out of Place: a Memoir*, London: Granta.

Said, E. (2000), *Reflections on Exile*, London: Granta Books.

Samuel, R. (1989), *Patriotism: The Making and Unmaking of British National Identity*, 3 vols, London: Routlege.

Sayad, A. (2004), *The Suffering of the Immigrant*, preface by Pierre Bourdieu, translated by David Macey, Oxford: Polity Press.

Schultheis, F. and Frisinghelli, C. (2004), *Pierre Bourdieu: In Algeria. Testimonies of Uprooting*, Graz: Camera Austria.

Schwarz, B. (1996), *The Expansion of England: Race, Ethnicity and Cultural History*, London: Routledge.

Scott, J. (1990), *The Sociology of Elites*, Aldershot: Elgar.

Scott, J. (1991), *Who Rules Britain?* Oxford: Polity Press.

Segal, L. (1997), *Slow Motion: Changing Masculinities: Changing Men*, London: Virago.

Seidler, V. (1989), *Rediscovering Masculinity: Reason, Language and Sexuality*, London: Routledge.

Sharma, S., Hutnyk, J. and Sharma, A. (eds) (1996), *Dis-Orienting Rhythms: The Politics of the New Asian Dance Music*, London: Zed Books.

Sharp, J.P. (1996), 'Gendering Nationhood', in N. Duncan (ed.) *Body Space: Destabilizing Geographies of Gender and Sexuality*, London: Routledge.

Shaw, S. (2002), *Language and Gender in Political Debates in the House of Commons*, London: The Institute of Education, University of London.

Sibley, D. (1997), *Geographies of Social Exclusion: Society and Difference in the West*, London: Routledge.

Sibley, D. (1998), 'The Racialisation of Space in British Cities', *Soundings* 10: 119–27.

Simmonds, F. (1997), 'My Body, Myself: How Does a Black Woman Do Sociology?', in H. Mirza (ed.), *Black British Feminism*, London: Routledge.

Skeggs, B. (1997), *Formations of Class and Gender*, London: Sage.

Smith, Z. and Dodd, P. (2000), 'Capital Gains', *The Art Magazine*, 21: 36–42, London: Tate Gallery.

Solomos, J. and Back, L. (1995), *Race, Politics and Social Change*, London: Routledge.

Bibliography

Spelman, E. (1982), 'Woman as Body: Ancient and Contemporary Views', *Feminist Studies* 8 (1): 109–12.

Spivak, G.C. (1988a), 'Can the Subaltern Speak?', in C. Nelson and L. Grossberg (eds), *Marxism and the Interpretation of Cultures*, Urbana: University of Illinois Press.

Spivak, G.C. (1988b), *In Other Worlds: Essays in Cultural Politics*, London: Methuen.

Spivak, G.C. (1999), *A Critique of Postcolonial Reason: Toward a History of the Vanishing Present*, Cambridge, MA: Harvard University Press.

Spivak, G. (2001), 'Mapping the Present': Interview with M. Yegenoglu and M. Mutman, *New Formations* 45: 9–23.

Sreberny-Mohammadi, A. and Ross, K. (1996), 'Women MPs and the Media: Representing the Body Politic', in J. Lovenduski and N. Pippa (eds), *Women in Politics*, Oxford: Oxford University Press.

Stanworth, P. and Giddens, A. (1974), *Elites and Power in British Society*, London: Cambridge University Press.

Sunder Rajan, R. (1993), *Real and Imagined Women: Gender, Culture and Postcolonialism*, London: Routledge.

Taussig, M. (1997), *The Magic of the State*, London: Routledge.

Tazzi, P.L., Bhabha, H.K. and Kapoor, A. (1998) *Anish Kapoor*, London: Hayward Gallery and University of California Press.

Vallance, E. (1979), *Women in the House: a Study of Women Members of Parliament*, London: Athlone Press.

Wakeford, J. and Urry, S. (eds) (1973), *Power in Britain*, London: Heinemann Educational.

Walters, P. (1987), 'Servants of the Crown', in A. Spencer and D. Podmore (eds), *In a Man's World*, London: Tavistock Publications.

Warner, M. (1996), *Monuments and Maidens*, London: Vintage.

Warner, M. (2000), *No Go the Bogey Man*, London: Vintage.

Whitford, M. (1991), *The Irigaray Reader*, Oxford: Blackwell.

Williams, P. (1997a), *Reith Lecture*, BBC Radio 4.

Williams, P. (1997b), *Seeing a Color-Blind Future: the Paradox of Race*, London: Virago Press.

Williams, R. (1989), *What I Came To Say*, London: Hutchinson Radius.

Wilson, E. (1992), *The Sphinx in the City*, Berkeley: University of California Press.

Wilson, J.and Wilson, L. (1999), *Parliament*, The Serpentine Gallery, London.

Witz, A., Warhurst, C. and Nickson, D. (2003), 'The Labour of Aesthetics and the Aesthetics of Organization', *Organization* 10 (11): 33–54.

Wolkowitz, C. (2001), 'The Working Body as Sign: Historical Snapshots', in K. Backett-Milburn and L. McKie (eds), *Constructing Gendered Bodies*, Basingstoke: Macmillan.

Young, R. (1990), *White Mythologies: History and the West*, London: Routledge.

Young, R. (2000), 'Deconstruction and the Postcolonial', in N. Royle (ed.), *Deconstructions: a Users' Guide*, London: Palgrave.

Young, R. (2001), *Postcolonialism: A Historical Introduction*, Oxford: Blackwell Publishers.

Yuval-Davis, N. (1997), *Gender and Nation*, London: Sage.

Notes

Chapter 1 Introduction: Proximities

1. I am going to use the term 'black' to refer to those people who are associated with the African and South Asian diaspora. There has been a productive and contentious discussion of the use of the category 'black' as opposed to ethnic groupings in Britain (Hall 1989; Brah 1992; Mercer 1994). It could, of course, be argued that the meaning of the terms sex and gender have a similar, socially constructed, instability and ambiguity attached to their usage (Butler 1989, 1993a).
2. We can also be certain that the figure of the 'Unknown Soldier' won't be a Ram Das, Sawarn Singh or Rani Kapur; these non-white faces from the ex-colonies have been absolutely erased in the 'imagined community'. Thus we can't say that 'As the Unknown Soldier could potentially be any man who has laid down his life for his nation, the nation is embodied within each man and each man comes to embody the nation' (Sharp 1996: 99). We are talking about specific men. The nation and the citizen are racialised, as well as gendered, entities.
3. Journalists have conducted in-depth life-history interviews with women politicians (Phillips 1980; McDougall 1998). Because of the genre they are located in, they are atheoretical.

Chapter 2 Of Men and Empire

1. This figure continues to have a hold on the imagination of the nation. Winston Churchill is most famously associated with the Second World War and the defeat of Nazism. In a BBC public poll on 25 November 2002 he was named the greatest Briton of all time. His own thoughts on 'race' were avidly pro-empire and pro-Britannia.
2. The multiple and contradictory nature of modernity and enlightenment ideals have been emphasised by a range of thinkers who criticise the

homogeneous characterisation of modernity. Bhatt (2002) argues that enlightenment was not monolithic. European thought and that of other places were quite ambivalently interrelated. Schopenhauer, for instance, had much time for Hindu and Indian philosophy and yet he derided Jews.

3. Today Paul Gilroy wants to return to modernity's first principles via a 'planetary humanism'. But this is only after the 'exclusionary character of modernity's loudly trumpeted democratic aspirations has been flushed out of the cover provided by the inclusive, humanistic, rhetoric' (Gilroy 2000: 72).

4. Within political theory much more attention has been granted to gender than to 'race'. However, gender and 'race' have not been treated together by scholars who give equal weight to both, even though scholars procedurally list them together.

5. Mills does not lump all whites into one simple homogeneous category; for instance, he recognises the difference between the Irish (who are 'borderline whites') and the English. Taking this into account, he argues that there are demarcations within whites and blacks, so that 'some are whiter, and so more equal, than others, and all non-whites are unequal, but some are blacker, and so more unequal than others. The fundamental conceptual cut, the primary division, then remains that between whites and nonwhites, and the fuzzy status of inferior whites is accommodated by the category of "off-white" rather than nonwhite' (1997: 80).

6. Elizabeth Wilson (1992) has documented the ways in which the rise of urban spaces offered productive possibilities for women, as well as trangressive forms of masculinity, such as the flâneur.

Chapter 3 Dissonant Bodies

1. Interestingly, though, the work of Bhabha (1994), who is one of the most cited (and critiqued) postcolonial theorists in his much cited essays on 'Sly Civility' and 'Mimic Man', feature an Indian civil servant.

2. On 25 February 1999 the Press Office at The Commission for Racial Equality confirmed that a statement to this effect was made by Herman Ousely.

3. Discussions of what defines élites go back at the very least as far as Pareto and Livingston (1935) and Mosca and Livingston (1939) in political theory. The term is highly debated (Mills 1963; Domhoff 1967; Moyser and Wagstaffe 1987; Scott 1990; Bottomore 1993).

4. When I entered their art world, their life-size visuals resonated with my memory of conducting interviews with MPs within wood-panelled walls, echoing corridors, clattering tearooms, offices with the sound of Big Ben in the background (a constant reminder of the time they were giving me) and lobbies and bars, where the bell for voting would abruptly interrupt the flow of conversation.

5. While Fanon has spoken of women in specific, and often problematic, terms, I am using his discussion of 'race' for thinking about male and female experiences.

6. There is a long-standing and ever-evolving academic dispute over the theoretical and political placement of Fanon. Some have claimed him as a Marxist, others a black revolutionary, some locate the existentialist Fanon, while others see a potential fellow-Lacanian in the making. While these battles will no doubt continue to rage, I am not placing a definitive stamp on his corpus of works. For me, he brings an analytical tool-box that helps us to shed great light on everyday forms of racism, most especially as they are experienced in institutions. And, in this sense, his work is under-utilised.

7. Working in Algeria as a psychiatrist and activist with the forces against French imperialism in the war for independence, and think-ing of the people he grew up with in the Antilles, as well as the Senegalese armies who had passed through, Fanon operates with a wide and inclusive definition of 'black' or negro: one which includes, as he says, every 'colonized people' (1986: 18).

8. Gender also affects how the burden of doubt is allocated (see Chapter 5).

9. On 16 October 2003 the Cabinet Office announced that women represented 22.9% of the very top posts in the civil service and that 2.8% at senior levels in general are from minority ethnic backgrounds. Consult www.cabinet-office.gov.uk for the latest statistics at different levels of recruitment.

10. Robert Young notes Lévi-Strauss's anti-racism. He says:

> Lévi-Strauss disputed the noxious effects of the division, central to western notions of culture, between the civilized and the primitive, the masculine and the feminine, by demonstrating that so-called primitive logic was as valid, and as controlled in its method, as western rationalism itself (Lévi-Strauss 1968). The direction of his work was anti-eurocentric,

against the assumption of civilized superiority, of western difference. (2001: 420)

That said, Bourdieu locates a 'cavalier approach' to other cultures in the work of Lévi-Strauss and other anthropologists (1990b: 20). Even if the 'primitive' is valued and placed on an equal level, the very process in which the categorisations are derived can remain problematic.

11. This is not to say that the right to look has not been disturbed while it was 'out there' in the field, on the other side of the world. See Ann Oakley (1981) for a discussion of Evans-Pritchard's frustration with the 'natives'' unwillingness to cooperate.

12. Fields have been created in Mexico, the Amazon basin, Sweden, Britain and, most recently, China (which is the biggest field project to date, consisting of 190,000 pieces). For each of these, Gormley works with local communities to create thousands of figures. Each participant is instructed to mould a ball of clay which comfortably fits their hand (this could be a child or an adult), and to shape a figure who has two holes for eyes and stands up. These are then baked in a kiln.

13. Personal visit to *The Field for the British Isles* (exhibited at the British Museum 15 November 2002 to 26 January 2003). Gormley is represented by the White Cube Gallery, London.

14. It offers the potential both to de-centre the positionality of being a superior knower/leader and to further entrench boundaries. This is one of those moments where we could open the self to 'the incongruous and the unexpected', where 'we either fall into psychotic breakdown or rise to a poetics of new images and an ethics of new practices'. Kearney notes: 'For if each of us can accept that we are the strangers, then there are no strangers – only others like ourselves' (2003: 77).

15. Margaret Thatcher made a speech declaring that Britain is in danger of being 'swamped' by people of other cultures. The presence of these other cultures and people was represented as a terrorising, invading force that could annihilate what it was to be 'truly' British and English (Hall and Jacques 1983; Hall 1988). Today, in some quarters, most especially the metropolitan parts of the country, versions of the multicultural, however limited in themselves (Hesse 1999), are embraced as bringing variety and colour to a country. At the same time, though, there continues to be a sense in which the migrant and the refugee pose a threat. This could be a perceived as a threat to resources, for instance, jobs, even though many of them are

once again filling vacancies that are otherwise remaining unfilled, or it could be a threat to national security. In the light of 9/11 there has developed a frenzied attack in the press on asylum-seekers and long-standing Muslim migrants for being terrorists. In the 1970s the black male Afro-Caribbean figure was the violent mugger who was targeted as destroying the peace of the country (Hall, Jefferson, Clarke and Robert 1977); today, this figure is joined by the Muslim-looking terrorist.

Chapter 4   (In)Visible Universal Bodies

1. In *In Praise of Bureaucracy* Paul Du Gay has recently tried to recover a certain ethical dignity for the bureau and the bureaucrat. He praises the 'capacity to divorce the administration of public life from private moral absolutisms' (2000: x), and offers unwavering support for a 'legal-rational conduct of administration and the liberal-pluralist ethics of responsibility it embodies' (2000: 57). Du Gay does not engage with the problematic notions of universality and rights that the model he defends is commonly praised for widely in both public and theoretical political discourse.

2. All citations, unless stated otherwise, are from one hundred personal interviews conducted at Westminster and Whitehall with women and Black and Asian MPs and high-level civil servants for Project No. R000235450, funded by the Economic and Social Research Council (ESRC), titled 'New and Established Political Elites', directed by Professor John Scott at Essex University. To ensure maximum confidentiality the interviewees have not been named and to avoid identification through a process of delineation they have not been given individual numbers. The direct words of interviewees are located in quotation marks. Further details on the research are available from Puwar (1997a,b, 2000, 2001, 2004c).

3. A Higher Executive Officer is, incidentally, four grades below this interviewee's position.

4. The complexities involved in demarcating where the boundaries between insiders and outsiders are located and the notion of differentiated inclusion have several layers to them. Edward Said is, of course, in many ways an insider in academia. In specific radical quarters of cultural and political theory he is highly respected. He

is the postcolonial theorist. At the same time he knows the Western canon of literature, philosophy and music extremely well. However, it is not too much of an exaggeration to say that he is also despised by a significant number of people in the United States for his politics and links to the Middle East. But, even in academia, a world in whose language he is fully versed, he is, because of how he combines politics and academia in the role of a public intellectual, a bit of a maverick. When for instance the BBC asked him to deliver the Reith Lectures, there was significant discontent (Said 1994b).

5. This is a perfect form of Bentham's 'panopticon principle', observed by Foucault (1970), where the prisoner is always on his/her best behaviour because s/he never knows when the prison guards are watching her/him and could catch him out. Thus this threat means that in effect he guards himself and polices himself.

6. I am not in any way belittling the political power of autobiographical work or self-testimonies; these are absolutely essential for contesting histories, as well as for bringing to life what has been buried or in fact denigrated. However, testimonials have also been classically used to assign victimhood, paralleled by a politics of salvation.

Chapter 5 Performative Rites: Ill-fitting Suits

1. Sylvia Shaw (2002) rather unconventionally for the field of women and politics, applies conversational analysis to interactions and speech in the House of Commons. This qualitative approach has been seriously lacking in this area of research, which is overwhelmingly quantitative in its analysis even when it is reliant upon qualitative data.

Chapter 6 The Imperial/Legitimate Language

1. In our case this would be the 'Queen's English'.

2. This could be on the basis of gender, race, class, religion or any other social criterion that is more than the explicitly stated technical requirements. Bourdieu goes on to note: 'A number of official criteria in fact serve as a mask for hidden criteria: for example, the requiring of a given diploma can be a way of demanding a particular social origin.' Speaking more specifically, he says:

The members of groups based on co-option, as are most of the corps protected by an overt or covert numerus clausus (doctors, architects, professors, engineers etc.) always have something else in common beyond the characteristics explicitly demanded. The common image of the professions, which is no doubt one of the real determinants of 'vocations', is less abstract and unreal than that presented by statisticians; it takes into account not only the nature of the job and the income, but those secondary characteristics which are often the basis of their social value (prestige or discredit) and which, though absent from the official job description, function as tacit requirements, such as age, sex, social or ethnic origin, overtly or implicitly guiding co-option choices, from entry into the profession and right through a career, so that members of the corps who lack these traits are excluded or marginalized (women doctors and lawyers tending to be restricted to a female clientele and black doctors and lawyers to black clients or research). In short, the property emphasized by the name used to designate a category, usually a occupation, is liable to mask the effect of the secondary properties which, although constitutive of the category, are not expressly indicated. (Bourdieu 1984: 102–3)

3. The study of and struggle against racism were a key feature of Bourdieu's work. In his research laboratory he worked closely with Abdelmalek Sayad on questions of racism and migration, most especially in relation to France and Algeria (Bourdieu 1958; Bourdieu and Darbel 1963; Bourdieu and Sayad 1964). In fact, Bourdieu's earliest research, like the work of other influential thinkers, such as Althusser, Derrida and Cixious, was totally embroiled with issues of colonialism and racism (Young 2000: 191–3, 2001: 411–16). Many of these intellectuals were themselves located outside standard French society due to their exposure to the butt-end of colonialism in Algeria, especially during the Algerian war. They were not, as Young puts it, "'français de souche", "of good stock"' (2001: 415). Just before his death in 2002, Bourdieu put together an exhibition publication titled *Pierre Bourdieu: In Algeria. Testimonies of Uprooting* from his archive of photographs taken during his fieldwork in Algeria between 1958 and 1961 (Schultheis and Frisinghelli 2004).

4. Fanon and Bourdieu were in Algeria at the same time during the struggle for Algerian independence. While both of them were against French colonialism, Bourdieu was much more ambivalent over the Front de Libération Nationale (FLN) than Fanon. Bourdieu's position was closer to that of Memmi (Le Sueur 2001). Intellectually, there was also some distance between them. Jean-Paul Sartre was an ally of Fanon; in fact, he wrote the preface to *Wretched of the Earth*. Bourdieu, whose mentor was Raymond Aron, was critical of Sartre (Robbins 2000).

5. Interestingly, non-whites who can perform perfect English, for instance, Salman Rushdie, are more likely to be accepted and respected by the British élite. Their hybridity is of a much more acceptable/respectable nature than that of black kids who grow up in the inner cities and speak a regionalised working class form of English.

6. Here we can make a comparison with authors such as Salman Rushdie, who studied at Oxford, and Hanif Kureshi, who studied at King's College, London. Both of these writers are accepted and respected by the British literati.

7. Incidentally, in the previous chapters I noted how Irigaray states that the sedimented alignment of social characteristics with specific types of corporeality becomes destabilised by the menace posed by female bodies who mimic male bodies (Irigaray 1985a). And, although Irigaray does not explicitly engage with questions of 'race', her work can, as she herself states, be enabling for thinking about how difference can coexist and be respected without making the other the same, that is, without collapsing it into an epistemic framing which sees it either as an inversion of self or as a support (Irigaray 2000). It is no doubt possible to see the productive aspect of her work. However, in her text *Between East and West* (2002), she romanticises the East. She engages with the East to see the West. In many respects the critique Spivak (1988b) makes of Kristeva, of using the 'other', most especially Chinese women, to illuminate self becomes, rather disappointingly, applicable to Irigaray.

8. Butler accuses Bourdieu of falsely separating the linguistic and the social (1999: 123), even though he provides detailed studies of the ways in which the social terrain impinges upon how the body (mouth, lips and posture) is trained to utter. In a discussion that moves in and out of Austin, Derrida and Bourdieu, Butler desperately searches for the transformative. What interests her are the escapes. However, the subject-matter of Bourdieu's work – class – barely gets a look-in. When Butler does mention class, Bourdieu is seen to rather crudely harness it to markets. The body and the cluster of concepts he employs in its discussion – helix, habitus, doxa and dispositions – are acknowledged, but they are not married to class. By wrenching the theoretical tools developed by Bourdieu out of their own social context, Butler has herself committed an error. Bourdieu is a theorist who is able to offer us a sense of how those at the margins are made to feel odd, inadequate, stupid, lacking. And we must not underestimate how this conversation in itself bears transformative potential for those who are not privileged by class. But Butler does not go there. Class is invisible as a site of privilege.

9. Nandi Bhatia's (2003) analysis of the 1933 novel *Bengal Nights* by the famous European orientalist scholar and Indologist at the University of Chicago, Mircea Eliade, can be utilised to think of the case of colonised women. The novel is based on his recollections of his romance with Maitreyi Devi, a middle-class Bengali woman, in the 1930s, at whose house he stayed to study Indian philosophy with her father. Bhatia notes that in *Bengal Nights* he defines his own whiteness in contrast to her Indianness, which is constructed as 'primitive'. She notes that he dismisses her relatively advanced knowledge of philosophy, poetry, languages and arts as the mark of a child who has read too much, and constructs their relationship as that of civilised man and barbarian. I would like to extend Bhatia's analysis by saying that, when he is faced with an intellectual Indian woman who is able to converse in the discourse he wants to make his own, Eliade becomes tormented. These are again, in Bhabha's sense, the right words in the wrong mouth.

10. This is quite possibly a tension that results from Bhabha's use of Foucault's analysis of conditions of the power for looking at the colonial apparatus, coupled with the central place of the concept of ambivalence via Freud and Lacan on fetishism, which is then mapped on to agency in considering the anxiety, dissonance and failure of colonial control (Young 1990: 144).

11. Although the postcolonial context is markedly different from the colonial situation, there is some continuity in the moral psychology of these two contexts. Postcolonial scholars have paid particular attention to the endurance of cultural imperialism (Said 1994a). It is also important to bear in mind that the colonial civil service was not identical to the British civil service in existence today, though there are no doubt considerable overlaps, even if they are situated in different time frames (Harris 1991).

Chapter 7 Becoming Insiders

1. Whiteness, class and gender are usually studied historically (see Hall, C. 1992). Much less attention is paid to the contemporary moment.

2. I think the word 'travellers' can be useful for graphically thinking about space, territory and movement. However, the problem with

it is that it carries connotations of free movement, adventure and imperial expeditions. I prefer the term 'space invaders' because it emphasises bodies, borders and territorial protectionism even while there is change and movement.

3. I have borrowed the metaphor of the sponsor from the language of immigration, where sponsoring enables people from 'other' countries to enter Britain as legitimate and 'safe' entrants.

Chapter 8 In Summation

1. There are, of course, considerable comparative differences in the increase, depending on whether it is a question of gender or 'race'. Thus, whilst I have noted somewhat similar machinations of exclusion operating on the basis of both gender and race, it is also important to emphasise the differences, in terms of structural locations and the legitimacy of the issues.

2. Locating himself as belonging to two opposing ethnic identities, Said says, 'To be at the same time Wog and Anglican was to be in a state of standing civil war' (*Guardian*, Saturday Review, 11 September 1999).

Index

Index

Index

Index

Index

Index

Index